GENOCIDAL PEACE

Vladimir "Zerubbabel" Putin's Quest to Conquer the World
Daniel 8: 24, 25

by
John Bazzanella

Copyright

All rights reserved. No part of this publication may be reproduced, distributed, or transmitted in any form or by any means, including photocopying, recording, or other electronic or mechanical methods without the prior written permission of the author.

Copyright © 2025 by John Bazzanella
bazzanella413@yahoo.com.ph
www.johnbazzanellabooks.com
Printed in the United States of America

This book is dedicated to my lawyer Peter D. Mudry who refused to be my lawyer after I wanted to desperately go to CAMH (Center for Addiction and Mental Health) psychiatric institution in Toronto, Ontario, Canada. I regret coming to this CAMH psychiatric institution because of the abuse I had experienced at the hands of my caregivers. Where here in CAMH I experienced a stroke on May 8th / 2022 because of the psychiatric drug called "Invega" that causes blood clots. And I have been also blinded in my left eye because of the psychiatric drug called "Haldol." Both these drugs were forced on me by psychiatrist Dr. Maxym Choptiany and psychiatrist Dr. Georgia Walton and psychiatrist Dr. Shi Kai Liu by injection with security guards present if I did not accept these injections of Haldol and Invega.

Thank you, Peter Mudry for the years of support you gave to me. I will always remember you for your help and compassion during my difficult years in psychiatric institutions.

Sincerely --- John Bazzanella

CONTENTS

INTRODUCTION

Chapter 1: Flaws of Democracy

Chapter 2: What is Religion?

Chapter 3: What is Babylon?

Chapter 4: Who is God?

Chapter 5: Committing Genocidal Peace

Chapter 6: Desperate Dictators

Chapter 7: Haughty Psychology

Chapter 8: Haughtiness Spawns Humiliation

Chapter 9: Power of Humiliation

Chapter 10: Humility Destroys Destruction

Epilogue

Credits and Acknowledgements

INTRODUCTION

According to the five books that John Bazzanella has written that are titled "Pyromancy", "Open Tomb, Aviation 666, Monsters of Genesis", "Magistrates of Damnation", "Immunity from Prosecution", and "Ancient Blood of Violence" has made comments in his books about this civilization and it's corrupt political and social and economic conditions that have plagued humanity into a suffering state of affairs on a worldwide scale. Not only on a domestic and national level but on an international level as well.

John Bazzanella has also made quotes from a Biblical perspective that would get you crucified in the face of these world leaders in each and every country. Christ was crucified for speaking out against the apostate religious authorities of his time claiming to be the Son of God according to Matthew 27 : 11, 12, 13, 14, 15, 16, 17, 18, 19, 20, 21, 22 and John 10: 31, 32, 33. Here the world has never learned how to acknowledge God since the crucifixion of Christ; regarding this "atrocious rejection of God mentality" that still exists in our world today. And it comes as no surprise that man has never learned his lesson to having the knowledge of God and humility and a reverential fear of God according to Proverbs 1: 29, 30 and Proverbs 22: 2, 3, 4.

Also the middle name that John Bazzanella gave Vladimir Putin which is "Zerubbabel" is a name that is symbolic or represents Babylon or is from Babylon according to Ezra 4: 1, 2, 3, 4, 5, 6 , 11, 12, 13. Which Babylon here is also known as confusion according to the Strong's Exhaustive Concordance of the Bible # 2216 from # 2215 and # 894 that refers to "Zerubbabel" as descended of Babylon or to flow away --- wax warm or confusion ; Babel (i.e. Babylon). Here Vladimir Putin's usage of his Orthodox Christian faith is to judge the world and perhaps judge those true servants of God. Who here also is that Putin has apostate religious beliefs according to 2nd Corinthians 11: 13, 14, 15 and neglecting political prudent leadership and having covetous mindset and oppressing the righteous and the poor according to Proverbs 28: 14, 15, 16. And where John Bazzanella may be sentenced to a furnace after Putin is claiming that John Bazzanella has caused this so called perdition of civilization; as Putin may be claiming according to his Babylonian Apostate Religious beliefs and roots. Claiming perhaps that John Bazzanella has caused division of a One World Government that Putin plans to bring about and conquer and his rule and desire to save the world. And that Putin may be also claiming that John Bazzanella has caused perdition of civilization according to John 17: 12 because of the books John Bazzanella has written and that John Bazzanella has had published. And that these books may be now influencing humanity to reject this One World Government that Putin plans to bring about with perhaps the aid of a coming authoritarian leader of the United States under possibly the coming U.S. Presidency and Administration of Donald Trump in November 2024.

CHAPTER 1
Flaws of Democracy

What are the flaws of Democracy? What are the disadvantages when it comes to Democracy? The Democratic structure of the government like political polarization, racial tension, identity politics, money politics, social divide, and income disparity are among some of the issues that have gotten worse in the past few decades according to 2nd Timothy 3: 1, 2, 3, 4, 5. Also income disparity is a big problem which causes an imbalanced economic condition that may also lead to violence against those who are the proprietors of a business being the victims of their employees who may be disgruntled about their finances and wages where some shootings may have happened at their workplace of employment.

Some of these shootings may have also been done by the perpetrators who were victims of financial burdens in our society. Or it could have been for social conflict or racist reasons, or the perpetrators of these shootings may have also been outcasts or lone wolves in the community. There have been many shootings, and these are only workplaces of employment. Not to mention school shootings or mall shootings or sports or concert venue shootings that have occurred. And also, social gatherings of many people of events and parties that have taken place, whether private or public places where these shootings have also occurred.

Here are examples of some of these many workplace shootings that has happened in the U.S. and not to even mention Canada or other countries. That here to mention more countries or other shootings in other parts of the world would be totally redundant. So here are these shootings in the U.S. to only mention a few here sarcastically speaking.

Like the Louisville Bank shooting in Louisville Kentucky in 2023 leaving 5 dead and 8 injured.

The Buffalo supermarket massacre, Buffalo New York in 2022 leaving 10 dead and 3 injured.

The Virginia Walmart shooting, Chesapeake, Virginia in 2022 leaving

6 dead and 6 injured.

Boulder supermarket shooting, Boulder, Colorado in 2021 leaving 10 dead and none injured.

San Jose VTA shooting, San Jose California in 2021 leaving 9 dead and none injured.

Atlanta massage parlor shootings, Atlanta, Georgia in 2021 leaving 8 dead and 1 injured.

FedEx warehouse shooting Indianapolis, Indiana in 2021 leaving 8 dead and 7 injured.

El Paso Walmart mass shooting, El Paso Texas in 2019 leaving 22 dead and 26 injured.

Virginia Beach municipal building shooting, Virginia Beach, Virginia in 2019 leaving 12 dead and 4 injured.

Harry Pratt Co. warehouse shooting, Aurora, Illinois in 2019 leaving 5 dead and 6 injured.

Excel Industries mass shooting, Hesston Kansas in 2016 leaving 3 dead and 14 injured.

Planned Parenthood clinic shooting, Colorado Springs, Colorado in 2015 leaving 3 dead and 9 injured.

Lockheed Martin shooting, Meridian, Mississippi in 2003 leaving 7 dead and 8 injured.

Atlanta day trading spree killings, Atlanta Georgia in 1999 leaving 9 dead and 13 injured.

Standard Gravure shooting, Louisville Kentucky in 1989 leaving 9 dead and 12 injured.

United States Postal Service mass shooting, Edmond, Oklahoma in 1986 leaving 15 dead and 6 injured.

Hartford Beer Distributor shooting, Manchester, Connecticut in 2010 leaving 9 dead and 2 injured.

Goleta postal shootings, Goleta, California in 2006 leaving 8 dead and none injured.

Navistar shooting, Melrose Park, Illinois in 2001 leaving 5 dead and 4 injured.

Accent Signage Systems shooting, Minneapolis, Minnesota in 2012 leaving 7 dead and 1 injured.

Hotel shooting, Tampa Florida in 1999 leaving 5 dead and 3 injured.

Half Moon Bay spree shooting, Half Moon Bay, California, in 2023 leaving 7 dead and 1 injured.

Caltrans Maintenance yard shooting, Orange, California in 1997 leaving 5 dead and 2 injured.

Royal Oak postal shootings, Royal Oak Michigan in 1991 leaving 5 dead and 5 injured.

ESL shooting, Sunnyvale California in 1988 leaving 7 dead and 4 injured.
Xerox killings, Honolulu, Hawaii in 1999 leaving 7 dead and none injured.

Capital Gazette shooting, Annapolis, Maryland in 2018 leaving 5 dead and 2 injured.

Fort Lauderdale revenge shooting, Fort Lauderdale, Florida in 1996 leaving 6 dead and 1 injured.

R.E. Phelon Company shooting, Aiken, South Carolina in 1997 leaving 4 dead and 3 injured.

Atlantis Plastics shooting, Henderson, Kentucky in 2008 leaving 6 dead and 1 injured.

Wakefield massacre, Wakefield, Massachusetts in 2000 leaving 7 dead and none injured.

Rite Aid warehouse shooting, Perryman, Maryland in 2018 leaving 3 dead and 3 injured.

Edgewood business park shooting, Edgewood Maryland in 2017 leaving 3 dead and 3 injured.

Walter Rossler Company massacre, Corpus Christi, Texas in 1995 leaving 6 dead and none injured.

Connecticut Lottery shooting, Newington, Connecticut in 1998 leaving 5 dead and 1 injured.

Greenwood Park Mall shooting, Greenwood, Indiana in 2022 leaving 3 dead and 2 injured.

Fifth Third Center shooting, Cincinnati, Ohio in 2018 leaving 3 dead and 2 injured.

Chuck E. Cheese's killings, Aurora, Colorado in 1993 leaving 4 dead and 1 injured.

Orange office complex shooting, Orange California in 2021 leaving 4 dead and 1 injured.

SunTrust bank shooting, Sebring Florida, in 2019 leaving 5 dead and none injured.

T&T Trucking shooting Bakersfield, California in 2018 leaving 5 dead and none injured.

Florida awning manufacturer shooting, Orlando Florida in 2017 leaving 5 dead and none injured.

San Francisco UPS shooting, San Francisco California in 2017 leaving 3 dead and 2 injured.

Molson Coors shooting, Milwaukee, Wisconsin in 2020 leaving 5 dead and none injured.

Springfield convenience store shooting, Springfield, Missouri in 2020 leaving 4 dead and none injured.

Tulsa medical building shooting, Tulsa Oklahoma in 2022 leaving 4 dead and none injured.

Concrete company shooting, Smiths burg, Maryland in 2022 leaving 3 dead and 1 injured.

Rural Ohio nursing home shooting Kirksville Ohio in 2017 leaving 3 dead and none injured.

Mercy Hospital shooting, Chicago Illinois in 2018 leaving 3 dead and none injured.

Yountville veterans home shooting, Yountville, California in 2018 leaving 3 dead and none injured.

Pennsylvania supermarket shooting, Tunkhannock Pennsylvania in 2017 leaving 3 dead and none injured.

And Jacksonville Dollar General store shooting, Jacksonville, Florida in 2023 leaving 3 dead and none injured.

This is an example as put forth and mentioned in the Authorized King James Version Bible regarding the love of many that will wax cold leading to hate and perilous and dangerous times of brutal violence that is now occurring which is only going to get worse according to Matthew 24: 10, 11, 12 and 2nd Timothy 3: 1, 2, 3, 4, 5.

The scheme that Vladimir "Zerubbabel" Putin has here ---- is to dupe the world with a strong deception into thinking that Russia is a victim of religious and political persecution. Because of the reasons of Putin perpetrating this deception, he has a dark past and he has a reputation for committing murder on some of his own people and other people from other countries and unjustly imprisoning citizens from other countries to use them as hostages for political purposes. And now he is more than ever trying to justify his reasons for invading Ukraine.

How does Putin deflect the attention of his populace away from the totality of this corruption in his government? You give the world something more terrifying like giving them "The West and NATO". Here the great people of Russia are putting nuclear missiles in eastern Europe aimed at Russia--- saying NATO is preparing to attack Russia. NATO is an existential threat to Russia. We are victims. We must fight back before it's too late. Suddenly this deception and propaganda has power to make most people become duped into forgetting about their inept or unfit and foolish president and his thieving, corrupt leadership and start thinking about the existential threats to Mother Russia that do exist. Only problem is that it is all a bunch of fabricated lies and propaganda to mislead and deflect the attention of Putin's people and the world away from any of these conspiracies to bring about a non-democratic One World Government --- but to bring about an Authoritarian One World Government of a tyrannical nature to promise a world of peace ruled by an iron fist. Eliminating terrorism and improving the economy and eliminating poverty and getting the populace of the world into believing that will have security. When in fact this security is a false narrative to make it appear that citizens of Russia and the world will benefit from this --- but in reality it is a scheme to have those in power prosper by a tyrannical mindset with gaining the advantage of securing their leadership and possessing the whole world to themselves --- but the Bible warns of this type of mentality where they may lose their own souls and face judgment from God after Christ comes back to set up his kingdom. And therefore, our real Jesus Christ of the Authorized King James Version Bible eliminates the kingdom of this One World Government of the Beast or Antichrist or also known as the Apostate Religious Babylonian kingdom of the Beast or Antichrist according to Matthew 16: 26, 27, 28 and Revelation 17: 12, 13.

Putin has been quoted as saying as mentioned in the media that U.S. president Biden is a threat to democracy. Biden himself may be accepting this criticism as he too may be part of this conspiracy to bring about a One World Government without the God of the Authorized King James Version Bible --- but bring about a One World Government having a One World Apostate Religious institution in this governing body of the Beast or Anti-Christ being the woman as mentioned symbolically as the Roman Catholic Church which is known as the Vatican which has its origins in Rome.

This woman is symbolically known as the Roman Catholic Church that sits upon many waters or influencing many people and governments around the world according to Revelation 17: 1. This Roman Catholic Church which is also a large powerful religious institution has influenced so many people including political parties and institutions all around the world is a Roman Catholic Church which is identified as the whore according to Revelation 17: 4, 5 that has rejected the God of the Authorized King James Version Bible. And that will commit genocide on the true Christians and those true people who are the true converts who were not well informed of the Authorized King James Version Bible; but are or will be faithful to the God of the Authorized King James Version Bible who will be the martyrs of this worldwide genocide perpetrated by the tyrannical politicians and magistrates of this world like Putin and Trump and Biden and other dictators from the ten global regions of the world being the ten kings of Revelation 17: 12 and according to Revelation 17: 5, 6, 7, 12, 13.

And this Roman Catholic Church also has the colors of the robes of the Roman Catholic priests and the Golden Cup as used by the priests at their apostate ceremonial sessions of worship to a God that does not exist but angers the God of the Authorized King James Version Bible for their apostasy and being an abomination against our God of the Authorized King James Version Bible according to Revelation 17: 4.

Don't kid yourself this is all worldwide propaganda of making Biden look like a president who is not democratic so that Putin and Trump can be accepted by the worldwide populace of most of the countries in the world. So here they use this tactic of claiming that Biden is a threat to democracy as a means to deceive the populace of the world citizens to bring about a One World Government without God.

But they have an apostate belief in a God that does not exist. Where this false God is only a good God of love and does not judge, since man does not believe that man brings on his own destruction which is an indirect judgment of our God of the Authorized King James Version Bible.

Here, our God has prophetic implications for humanity by using man's own will to carry out his judgments on those who have rejected him facing martyrdom according to Revelation 20: 4 and Revelation 6: 9, 10, 11 or who are of a wicked mindset facing hell or damnation of the Lake of fire according to Revelation 14: 9, 10, 11 and Revelation 20: 12, 13, 14, 15. And these who have this wicked mindset are saying that there is no hope in John Bazzanella who claims to be a servant of God and that John Bazzanella is a horrible virgin of Israel who has preached destruction and martyrdom and not peace to the world. And they say that there is peace when there is no peace.

And now there is famine in Israel affecting a half a million people because of the war perpetrated by Hamas as of this writing on December 23rd / 2023 according to Jeremiah 14: 13, 14, 15, 18, 19. And these political tyrants have forsaken the words of warning coming from the cold flowing waters that come from another place or like a mental institution where John Bazzanella's words are coming from --- and that these words are now and have been forsaken for years according to Jeremiah 18: 9, 10, 11, 12, 13, 14 and since writing my letters and emails from today going way back to 1984 that were also totally ignored and with my first letter written to the musicians of Coney Hatch in 1984.

And then letters and emails that followed after that to news journalists and anchor news personalities and celebrities to the media according to Isaiah 41: 1, 2, 3, 4, 5, 6. And books that I had written that followed after these letters and emails just recently written and that also more of these letters and emails that were also written dating back to 1984.

The wars in Ukraine and Israel have tethered the economic power of nations bringing prosperity decline to the masses of this planet. In this world, with its microcosms of global cultures aftershocks of every quake are deeply felt. When there is war, the heightened tensions spill into our communities around the world and in our politics and into our lives affecting our security bringing on violence to us on an unpredictable scale.

Though often described as either "pro-Israeli" or "pro-Palestinian," there has been a spectrum of belief and behavior on display at events laying bare the challenge of broad labels.

There are those pouring their energies into efforts to bring about a ceasefire. There are those doing everything they can to make sure hostages are not overlooked or forgotten. There are others focused on what they want the future to be in this region of Israel ----and the futile efforts of whether that there should be a free Palestine or an eliminated Hamas, at no matter what the cost is. There are demonstrations of solidarity against discrimination as hate crimes in our world rise, and as Pope Francis calls for peace on December 24th / 2023 saying the prince of peace who has had his birthplace in this worn torn region was once more rejected by the futile logic of war of this futile land dispute that has been going on ever since Israel became an uncertain state or country in 1948.

Here it brought on violence because of this land dispute between the Palestinians and Israelis and because of this violence. Here the sins of those more innocent in Israel have become the scapegoats for the sins of the world. And according to God is that their iniquities were pardoned by God according to Isaiah 40: 1, 2. While the rest of the world of Journalists and reporters and celebrities in the high places or mountains or hills shall be made low and that these Journalists and reporters or celebrities await judgment according to Isaiah 40: 3, 4, 5, 6, 7, 8. And these Celebrities whether being politicians or Journalists or Reporters or media personalities may be subjected to judgments that consists of the following which are perhaps being subjected to becoming a fugitive according to Jeremiah 51: 50 and Ezekiel 13: 16, 17, 18, 19, 20, 21, 22, 23 or either being subjected to martyrdom according to Jeremiah 51: 49 and Revelation 6: 9, 10, 11 and Revelation 20: 4 or they will take the Mark of the Beast or known as this one world digital currency and global citizenship I.D. and be damned in hell or the lake of fire forever according to Revelation 14: 9, 10, 11 and Revelation 20: 12, 13, 14, 15.

So, is democracy flawed? Democracy is not only flawed but has the flaws of being too soft on criminals who are guilty as sin. And at the same time they condemned the innocent criminals who were sentenced to harsh time for committing crimes that were done for a reason --- for example if a person was trying to help someone financially and then this person who was getting the help defrauds the person who was trying to help him financially and defrauding him for his life savings --- and the person who fell victim to this fraud turns around and decides to murder him? Should he go away for 25 years without parole?

Then also we have Authoritarian dictatorships around the world or have a socialistic government or a communistic mindset where owning property is prohibited by this type of government. And also, where the rations of food and commodities are not equal for the citizens vs. the government. Here the citizens are deprived of prosperity. Why does this deprivation exist? The government may want to secure its leadership and tyrannical means to control the citizens to prosper and have total control over the populace in their own country.

So therefore, democracy is too soft on the guilty and too hard on the innocent; and socialism has exaggerated control on their citizens taking away their rights to prosper and live in peace. Also, if you were to be easy on the citizens of your own country regarding permitting them to prosper to a certain limit through rations. And having laws that punish the guilty and set the innocent free --- you would have a government that is easy to govern without violent protests and bureaucratic red tape that would be so excessive that chaos would ensue in governing. That would be costing the citizens an excessive amount of taxes and causing the government to commit corruption because of the expenses posed not only on citizens but on government officials who are subject to limited salaries because of these expenses that have also led to inflation on a nationally domestic and international scale. Here if common sense in counselors in the government prevails then the government in a country or in the world is established without war or conflict according to Proverbs 15: 22.

But Religious controversy is a very big problem on this planet. Like Hamas and their brutality, Christianity can be threatening as well --- of what is called as an imposter of Christianity and threatening American democracy. Supporters of then President Donald Trump outside the US Capitol on January 6 / 2021 in Washington, here three men with their eyes closed and heads bowed, pray before a roughhewn wooden cross. Another man wraps his arms around a massive Bible pressed against his chest like a shield. All throughout the crowd, people wave "Jesus Saves " banners and pump their fists toward the sky. At first glance this scene look likes an outdoor church rally. But this event wasn't a revival; it was what some call a Christian revolt. These were people who stormed the US Capitol on January 6 / 2021, during an attempt to overturn the results of the 2020 presidential election.

This insurrection marked the first time many Americans realized the US is facing a burgeoning White Christian nationalist movement. This movement uses Christian language to cloak sexism and hostility towards Black people and non-White immigrants in its quest to create a White Christian America.

A report from a team of clergy, scholars and advocates --- sponsored by two groups that advocate for separation of church and state --- concluded that this ideology was used to bolster, justify and intensify the attack on the US Capitol. Much of the House January 6th Committee's focus so far has been on right wing extremist groups. But there are plenty of other Americans who have adopted teachings of the White Christian nationalists who stormed the Capitol often without knowing it, as Scholars, historians, sociologists and clergy have said.

White Christian nationalist beliefs have infiltrated the religious mainstream so thoroughly that virtually any conservative Christian pastor who tries to challenge its ideology risks their career, says Kristin Kobes Du Mez, author of the New York Times bestseller, "Jesus and John Wayne: How White Evangelicals Corrupted a Faith and Fractured a Nation." These ideas are so widespread that any individual pastor or Christian leader who tries to turn the tide and say, "Let's look again at Jesus and scripture," are going to be tossed aside, she says.

The ideas are also insidious because many sounds like expressions of Christian piety or harmless references to US history. But White Christian nationalists interpret these ideas in ways that are potentially violent and heretical. Their movement is not only anti- democratic, but it contradicts the life and teachings of Jesus Christ that some clergy and scholars and historians have said.

Samuel Perry, a professor of religious studies at the University of Oklahoma who is an authority on ideology, calls it an "imposter Christianity." Here are three key beliefs often tied to White Christian nationalism. A belief that the US was founded as a Christian nation. One of the of banners were spotted at the January 6 insurrection was a replica of the American flag with the caption "Jesus is My Savior, Trump is My President." Erasing the line separating piety from politics is a key characteristic of White Christian nationalism. Many want to reduce or erase the separation of church and state, say those who study the movement. One of the most popular beliefs among White Christian nationalists is that the US was founded as a Christian nation; the Founding Fathers were all orthodox, evangelical Christians; and God has chosen the US for a special role in history.

These beliefs are growing among Christians, according to a survey done last year by the Barna Group, a company that conducts surveys about faith and culture for communities of faith and nonprofits. The group found that an "increasing number of American Christians believe strongly " that the US is a Christian nation, has not oppressed minorities, and has been chosen by God to lead the world. But the notion that the US was founded as a Christian nation is bad history theology, says Philip Gorski, a sociologist at Yale University and co-author of "The Flag and the Cross: White Christian Nationalism and the Threat to American Democracy." It's a half truth, and a mythological version of American history," Gorski says. Some Founding Fathers did view the founding of the nation through a Biblical lens, Gorski says, (Every state constitution contains a reference to God or the divine). But many did not. And virtually none of them could be classified as evangelical Christians. They were a collection of atheists, Unitarians, Deists and liberal Protestants and other denominations and secular in nature and possibly being in numbers as the god of this world according to 2nd Corinthians 4: 3, 4.

Here they are claiming that either Jesus Christ is their savior or that Donald Trump is their savior or that he is taking the place of the savior of the Authorized King James Version Bible who is the real Jesus Christ who came in the flesh to save mankind from their sins. Also, Donald Trump was known as mentioned in the media to sign Bibles and putting his name and signature to a divine book. Here Trump may be accepted and received as that savior who is an imposter of the real Jesus Christ of the Authorized King James Version Bible according to 2nd Thessalonians 2: 4. And that most Christians will accept him or receive him who are secular in nature and obsessed with money and riches according to John 5: 43, 44. The constitution also says nothing about God, the Bible or the Ten Commandments, Gorski says. And saying the US was founded as a Christian nation ignores the fact that much of its initial wealth was derived from slave labour and land stolen from Native Americans he says.

For evidence that the United States was as a secular nation, look no further than the 1797 Treaty of Tripoli, an agreement the US negotiated with a country in present-day Libya to end the practice of pirates attacking American ships. It was ratified unanimously by a Senate still half filled with signers of the Constitution and declared, the government of the United States of America is not, in any sense, founded on Christian religion.

It is peculiar that the notion of being a Christian has the stereotypical sense of having morals when in fact in some cases the opposite is true that hypocrisy is a characteristic trait of some Christians who claim to be faithful to God but in the end they are professing Christians and are reprobates concerning the faith and have the mindset of a secular nature and supporting a secular apostate Christian former US president like Donald Trump who may become that dictator or Antichrist or Beast of a coming One World Government according to Titus 1: 10, 11, 12, 13, 14, 15, 16 and Revelation 17: 12, 13.

Does this mean that any White Christian who salutes the flag and says they love their country is a Christian nationalist? No not at all historians say. A White Christian who says they love America, and its values and institutions is not the same thing as a White Christian nationalist scholars say. Gorski also notes that many devout Black Americans have exhibited a form of patriotism that does not degenerate into Christian nationalism. Gorski points to examples of the 19th century abolitionist, Frederick Douglas, and the Rev. Martin Luther King Jr. Both were devout Christians who expressed admiration for America and its founding documents. But their patriotism also meant that "they challenged the nation to live up to its highest principles, to become a place of freedom, equality, justice and inclusion," he says. And that also the injustice that the Bible speaks of in secular Government had Martin Luther King assassinated for his values and moral beliefs against a corrupt secular government according to Psalms 82: 1, 2, 3, 4, 5 and Ecclesiastes 5: 8, 9, 10.

Here Gorski also says that the Patriotism of White Christian nationalists, on the other hand, is a form of racial tribalism. They say "It's my tribe. We (white people) were here first. This is our country, and we don't like people who are trying to change it or people who are a different form of nationalism, Gorski says. Here also the Bible points out that we should live peaceably with all men if it is possible at all costs according to Romans 12: 16, 17, 18.

A belief in a Warrior Christ? Videos from the January 6 attack show a chaotic, tear gas- soaked scene at the Capitol that looked more like a medieval battle. Insurrectionists punched police officers, used flagpoles as spears and smashed officers' faces against doors while a mob chanted, "Fight for Trump!". The attack left five people dead and nearly 140 law enforcement officers injured in the midst of Trump's efforts to be elected once again to the presidential office of the United States, and in his midst, violence erupted because of his possible defeat that was emerging in the electoral process and that violence ensued in Donald Trump's midst according to Ezekiel 28: 16.

The incongruity of people carrying "Jesus Saves" signs while joining a mob whose members are pummeling police officers leads to an obvious question: How can White Christian nationalists who claim to follow Jesus, the "Prince of Peace" who renounced violence in the Gospels, support a violent insurrection? Here seditions and hatred and wrath and strife that is done by those people who are trying to overthrow the government will not inherit the Kingdom of God as mentioned in the Authorized King James Version Bible according to Galatians 5: 20, 21.

The reason for this sedition, hatred, wrath, strife, is because they follow a different Jesus than the one depicted in the Gospels, says Kristin Kobes Du Mez who is a professor of history and gender studies at Calvin University --- A Christian school --- in Michigan. They follow the Jesus depicted in the Book of Revelation, the warrior with eyes like "flames of fire" and "a robe dipped in blood" who led the armies of heaven on white horses in a final triumphant battle against the forces of the antichrist. White Christian nationalists have refashioned Jesus into a kick-butt savior who is willing to smite enemies to restore America to a Christian nation by force, if necessary, Du Mez and others say. While war like language like putting on the full armor of God has long been common in Christian sermons and hymns, it has largely been interpreted as metaphorical which really refers to and means that putting on the full armor of God is to resist immoral acts done against God's ordinances and statutes and judgments.

But many White Nationalists take that language of these metaphors literally in a sense of rebellion and seditions. Here these White Christian nationalists will say to those who are truly faithful who are the lost sheep of the real Christ of the Authorized King James Version Bible that we offend not to judge these lost sheep who belong to the real Christ have devoured them by martyrdom because they have sinned against the Lord, the habitation of justice as they claim which they believe is the hope of their Babylonian White Christian nationalists fathers according to Jeremiah 50: 7. But murdering a Brethren without a cause who has their faith as lost sheep in Christ shall be in danger of the judgment according to Matthew 5 : 20, 21, 22. Therefore let every man be judged by God according to Hebrews 9: 26, 27.

This violence was clear on January 6. Some insurrectionists wore caps emblazoned with "God, Guns, Trump and chanted that the blood of Jesus" was washing Congress clean. One wrote "In God We Trust" on a set of gallows erected at the Capitol. "They want the warrior Christ who wields a bloody sword and defeats his enemies", says Du Mez. They want to battle with that Jesus. That Jesus brings peace, but only after he slays his enemies. "And that Jesus sanctions or implements or determines moral judgment with the use of righteous violence if a government opposes God she says."

If you deem somebody in power to be working against the goals of a Christian America, then you should not submit to that authority and you should displace that authority, she says. "Because the stakes are so high, that the end justifies the means." That ends -justify-the means approach is a key part of White Christian nationalism, says Du Mez. It's why so many rallied behind former President Trump on January 6. She says he embodies a militant White masculinity that condones callous displays of power and appeals to Christian nationalists.

But with few exceptions White Christians nationalists are also hypocritical since at the same time they do not accept this militant masculinity when exhibited by Black, Middle Eastern and Latino men, Du Mez writes in "Jesus and John Wayne. Here aggression by people of color" is seen as a threat to the stability of home and nation she writes. I John Bazzanella believe that this hypocrisy is also similar to that hypocrisy of the Pharisees and the Jews according to Mark 7: 5, 6, 7, 8 and John 8: 37, 38, 39, 40, 41, 42, 43, 44, 45, 46, 47, 48, 49, 50, 51, 52, 53, 54, 55 ,56, 57, 58, 59.

Wisconsin Republican Senator Ron Johnson echoed this double standard and hypocrisy last year when he said on a radio talk show that he never really felt threatened by the mostly White mob that stormed the Capitol on January 6th. Now had .... President Trump won the election and those were tens of thousands of Black Lives Matter and Antifa protestors, "I might have been a little concerned," Johnson said.

I John Bazzanella has to laugh here --- so do those who are the critics of this Republican Senator Ron Johnson who has the audacity to make these claims with having outright hypocrisy. Later Johnson said, "there was nothing racial about my comments --- nothing whatsoever."

This embrace of a warrior Christ has shaped some White evangelicals' attitudes on issues ranging from political violence to gun safety laws. A survey last year by the Public Religion Research Institute revealed that of all respondents, White evangelicals were the religious group most likely to agree with the statement, "true American patriots might have to resort to violence to save the country."

Here there are also some White Christian nationalists who believe the Second Amendment was handed down by God. Samuel Perry, co-author of "Taking America Back for God: Christian Nationalism in the United States," wrote in a recent essay that among Americans surveyed who believe that "The federal government should declare the United States a Christian nation," over two thirds rejected the idea that federal government should enact stricter gun laws. Here those who are unjust are more in numbers being two thirds more in numbers being (the god of this world with a small "g") according to comparing those who are just, as mentioned in 2nd Corinthians 4: 4 and there is also an abominable conflict among the just and unjust according Proverbs 29: 27. Also there are those White Christians nationalists that are the false teachers of prophecy and morals according to 2nd Peter 2: 1, 2, 3. Here, the more you line up with Christian nationalism, the less likely you are to support gun control wrote Perry. Guns are practically an element of worship in the church of White Christian nationalism. A belief that there is such a person as a real American.

In the 2008 presidential election, vice presidential candidate Sarah Palin introduced a new term to the political discourse. She talked about "the real America" and the "pro -America areas of this great nation." Since then, many conservative political candidates have used the term "Real Americans" to draw contrasts between their supporters and their opposition. Here is a real example of division according to Proverbs 29: 27. Such Language has been co-opted into a worldview held by many White Christian nationalists: The nation is divided between "Real Americans" and other Citizens who don't deserve the same rights experts on White Christian Nationalism say.

Here also White Christian nationalists in the end times will fill the courtrooms with the slain by those who possess guns according to Ezekiel 9: 5, 6, 7, 8, 9 and according to Jeremiah 51: 49. This has brought me to tears as I write here for the slain who were good people who gave up their lives for Christ. Here the wicked carry out the judgments of God on Israel the wife of Jehovah who rejected God in the beginning because we are all in the dark about the Authorized King James Version Bible. But they accepted God in the end when it was too late to be saved physically as they ate and drank and had sex being in the flesh and being killed or crucified for Christ according to Galatian 2: 20 and Revelation 20: 4 and Revelation 6: 9, 10, 11. While the White Christian nationalists worship the coming Antichrist or Beast who may be Donald Trump or his successor and receive their Global citizenship I.D. and One World Government digital currency and their judgment is hell or the lake of fire according to Revelation 14: 9, 10, 11 and Revelation 17: 12, 13 and Revelation 13: 14, 15, 16, 17, 18 Revelation 20: 12, 13, 14, 15.

Gorski, author of "The Flag and the Cross," says he found in his research a strong correlation between White Christian nationalism and support for gerrymandering or giving special advantage or attention to one group or party or political unit for election advantage purposes also an electoral process where politicians manipulate district lines to favor one party or, some critics say, race over another. He found similar support among White Christian nationalists for the Electoral College, which gives disproportionate political power to many rural, largely White areas of the country. When White Christian nationalists claim an election was stolen, they are reflecting the belief that some votes don't count, he says.

It's the idea that we are the people, and our vote should count, and you're not the people, and .... you don't really deserve to have a voice, Gorski says. It doesn't matter what the voting machines say, because we know that all real Americans voted for Donald Trump.

Here White Christian nationalism is a threat to democracy. Those who want the US to become a Christian nation face a huge obstacle: Most Americans don't subscribe to their vision of America. Here the mainstream of White Christian nationalism comes as a growing number of Americans are rejecting organized religion. For the first time in the US last year, membership in communities of worship fell below 50%. Belief in God is at an all-time low, according to a recent Gallup poll and that there shall come a falling away of the true word of God that is preached and worshipped according to the Authorized King James Version Bible in 2nd Thessalonians 2: 1, 2, 3.

Add to that country's growing racial and religious diversity. People who identify as white alone declined for the first time since the census began in 1790, and many majorities of Americans under 18 are now people of color. On the surface, White Christian nationalism should not be on the ascent in America. So White Christian nationalists look for salvation from two sources. One is the embolden conservative majority on the US Supreme Court, where recent decisions overturning Roe vs. Wade and protecting school prayer offer them hope. Critics on the other hand, say the high court is eroding the separation of church and state. Not all Christians who support the high court's overturning of Roe vs. Wade and its school prayer decision are White nationalists. For example, plenty of Roman Catholics of all races support racial justice yet also backed the overturning of Roe. Here Roman Catholicism is apostate in nature and against the Bible, since the Authorized King James Version Bible supports abortion according to Jeremiah 20: 17, 18.

But White Christian nationalists are inspired by those decisions because one of their central goals is to erase the separation of church and state in the US. A recent study concluded that five of the justices on the Supreme Court are the "most pro-religion since at least World War II," and that the six conservative justices are all Christian, mostly Catholic, and not Biblically devout but religiously devout ---- I mean Biblically as referring to not being faithful to the Authorized King James Version Bible ---- but having a religious apostate nature of beliefs in the Biblical scriptures of any Bible or adhering to a specific Bible that may not be the Authorized King James Version Bible which has the authority of the word of God in ancient records that have been not altered in its translation --- while other versions of the Bible have corrupt translations.

While some Americans fear the dangers of one-party rule, others like Pamela Paul, a columnist, warn of the Supreme Court instituting a one-religion rule. With their brand of religious dogma losing its purchase, they're imposing it on the country themselves, she wrote in a recent New York Times editorial. Gorski, the historian says White Christian nationalism represents a grave threat to democracy because it defines "we the people" in a way that excludes many Americans. The United States cannot be both a truly multicultural democracy -- a people of people and a nation of nations --- and White Christian nation at the same time, "Gorski wrote in" The Flag and the Cross. "This is why White Christian nationalism has become a serious threat to democracy, perhaps the most serious threat it now faces."

The other source of hope for White Christian nationalists is a former occupant of the White House. Their devotion to him is illustrated by one of most striking images from the January 6 insurrection: A sign depicting a Nordic- looking Jesus wearing a red "Make America Great Again" hat. If Trump returns to the presidency, some White Christian nationalists may interpret his political resurrection as divine intervention. His support among White evangelicals increased from 2016 to 2020. Here Donald Trump may be accepted as a savior of the Middle East and the Israel and Hamas war and Ukraine war by putting it to an end and the crisis surrounding these issues --- he will be accepted as a leader sent by divine ordinance but will be a feign Christ in nature or may appear to be good in appearance until he is elected as a world leader and turns on humanity as a tyrant or a Beast or Antichrist bringing on tribulation in the world according to Matthew 24: 15, 16, 17, 18, 19, 20, 21, 22, 23, 24.

This insurrection is an attack that the Bible goes against since these insurrectionists are apostate Christians not faithful to the word of God committing seditions to overthrow Magistrates and Government and committing violence when they should be working for peace towards all men according to Romans 12: 16, 17, 18 and Galatians 5: 19, 20, 21, 22, 23.

And what men carrying wooden crosses among the Capitol mob couldn't achieve on January 6/ 2021, they might yet accomplish in 2024.

CHAPTER 2
What is Religion?

Since the time of Genesis God has paid a visit to man on a number of occasions. First it was at the time of Adam and Eve in the Garden of Eden when Eve committed the first sin leading Adam to committing sin as well according to Genesis 3: 8, 9, 10, 11, 12, 13. As time went on perhaps in the span of centuries God had the Sons of God visit planet earth to teach man the morals of God and teach man skills of survival according to Genesis 6: 1, 2, 3, 4. But these Sons of God had committed intercourse with the daughters of men on planet earth and begat newborns that were a corrupt offsprings since God had forbidden these immortal Sons of God not to mate with the terrestrial daughters of men since these Sons of God were extraterrestrial Sons of God. And this mating produced these births that resulted in these offsprings that would grow up to be Giants according to Genesis 6: 4.

After these Giants were born violence began to take place on planet earth in that early period of Genesis according to Genesis 6: 5. God during that period when the Sons of God visited earth had revealed himself through the existence of these Sons of God who had visited earth. Therefore, during that ancient period in Genesis, the daughters of men were not in the dark about the existence of God but were possibly deceived by these Sons of God by temptation knowing that both Adam and Eve knew they were sinning against God therefore that was the reason that they were judged by God being expelled from the Garden of Eden. And so God revoked Adam and Eve's immortality causing them to labour to till the ground to grow food being now mere mortals, according to Genesis 3: 17, 18, 19, 23, 24. This was also the reason for this judgment by God that it was because it was the same way that the daughters of men were deceived by the Sons of God who also sinned and disobeyed God. And were judged for trying to become like God knowing good and evil and also Eve was deceived by that Serpent in the Garden of Eden where this Serpent claimed that we can become Gods knowing good and evil if we eat from the knowledge of the tree of good and evil according Genesis 3: 1, 2, 3, 4, 5. Also the Sons of God who were known as the angels of God who fell into sin against God who were also Judged for mating with the daughters of men leaving their own estate and habitation that was given by God from somewhere in the cosmos as mentioned in and according to Jude 6.

For 2,000 years since the first coming of Christ to earth who was to be sacrificed for the sins of mankind, God has been silent. And after the ministry and death of Jesus Christ; man began to veer from the word of God and began creating his own system of doctrines from the revelations and word of God. Here today we have a multitude of different Religions that even date back before the time of Christ and in some cases, we have some Religions that date as far back as to the ancient times of Genesis or just shortly thereafter.

There is a documented source titled "Who is God?". Here a quote from this documented source that claims that God is only a loving God where his will to judge mankind is not mentioned claiming that we are a being with a God Spirit that indwells the mortal intellect and I now will be quoting this source as the following from "The Urantia Book":

"God is a Father in the highest possible sense of that term. He is eternally motivated by the perfect idealism of divine love and tender nature that finds its strongest expression and greatest satisfaction in loving and being loved. Selflessness is inherent in parental love. The first Father is universal spirit, eternal, truth, infinite reality, and father personality --- transcendent reality. But God is even more. He is a saving person and loving father to all who enjoy spiritual peace on Earth and who crave to experience personality survival in death. The existence of God is utterly beyond all possibility of demonstration, except for the God- consciousness of the human mind and the presence of the God- Spirit that indwells the mortal intellect --- and is bestowed as the free gift of the Universal Father. It is not there by right of possession, but it is designed to be so for all those who choose to survive the mortal existence." Unquote.

This Urantia Book introduces the word "Urantia" as the name of the planet "Earth" and states that its intent is to present enlarged concepts and advanced truth. This book aims to unite Religion and Science and Philosophy based on humanism. Here this refers to the apostasy and secularism that our world possesses that is influenced by a humanistic approach. This humanistic approach is based on loving all humans --- which is true. But have no fellowship with evil according to 2nd Corinthians 6 : 12, 13, 14, 15, 16. Here idols are also the bodies of the universe like planets or going out of our way to explore them since God is against this mindset of thinking and planning according to Obadiah 3, 4. We do not accept the judgments of God as Christ accepted these judgments according to Deuteronomy 32: 39. A secular mindset refuses to accept these Commandments and Statutes implemented by God according to Deuteronomy 11: 32.

The Roman Catholic religion and religious concept in its architectural structures can be found in the structures we have today in government buildings and the buildings that hold hearings and court proceedings and has a trace of its history of the ancient Roman temples that were among the most important buildings in Roman culture and the religious Roman Catholic institutions in the ancient period of the Roman Empire. And some of the richest buildings in Roman architecture, though only a few have survived in any sort of complete state. Today they remain "the most obvious symbol or Roman architecture." Their construction and maintenance were a major part of Ancient Roman Religion. And all towns of any importance had at least one main temple, as well as smaller shrines. The main room or also known as "cella" or "naos." Also, the inner chamber of an ancient Greek or Roman temple was also in classical antiquity. Its enclosure within walls has given rise to extended meanings, of a hermit's or monk's cell, and since the 17th century, was for a biological cell in plants and animals. Also, this main room known as "cella" housed the cult image of the deity which was the Roman deities most widely known today are those of the Romans who identified with Greek counterparts, integrating Greek myths, iconography, and sometimes religious practices into Roman Culture, including Latin literature, Roman art and religious life as it was experienced.

Also, the structures or buildings with these similar architecture designs and features related to the Roman or Religious architecture of the deities of the Ancient Roman Catholic religion such as large pillars amounted to thousands of examples like the White House, Buckingham Palace and St. Peters, Rome, and in recent years the temple front has become fashionable in China as well.

Here Renaissance and later Architects worked out ways of harmoniously adding high raised domes, towers and spires above a colonnaded temple portico front, something the Romans would have found odd. The Roman temple front remains a familiar feature of a subsequent Early Modern architecture in the Western Tradition, but although very commonly used for churches, it has lost the specific association with religion that it had for the Romans. Generally, later adaptions lack the colour of the original, and though there may be sculpture filling the pediment in grand examples, the full Roman complement of sculpture above the roofline is rarely emulated or to strive to equal or excel.

Variations on the theme, mostly Italian in origin, include: San Andrea, Mantua, 1462 by Leon Battista Alberti, which took a four columned Roman triumphal arch and added a pediment above; San Giorgio Maggiore, Venice, begun in 1566, by Andrea Palladio, which has two superimposed temple fronts, one low and wide, the other tall and narrow, the Villa Capra "La Rotunda", 1567 on, also by Palladio with four isolated temple fronts on each side of a rectangle, with a large central dome. In Baroque architecture two temple fronts, often of different orders, superimposed one above the other, became extremely common for Catholic churches often with the uppermost one supported by huge volutes to each side. Here "volutes" are a spiral, scroll -like ornament that forms the basis of the Ionic order, found in the capital of the Ionic column. It was later incorporated into Corinthian order and Composite column capitals. Four are normally to be found on Ionic capital, eight on Composite capitals.

I think I have made my point here regarding how church monuments and government building monuments have that church and religious architecture features that have since ancient times to the present infiltrated this type of architecture throughout the whole world. Where here religious devotion became so secular that Christ and Biblical stories like the birth of Christ and the Christmas tree became an origin of secular worship complete with Christmas and religious ornaments like "Angel ornaments" or stars like the "Star of David ornament" on a Christmas tree or a secular ornament like "Santa Claus and his reindeer", etc. since this religious secularism is all in vain according to Jeremiah 10: 1, 2, 3, 4.
What is Religion? The term is so broad that it includes all the deities of different cultures, different languages, different people who possess

different beliefs, and also different levels of intelligence that invites either the absolute truth of a deity or the absolute falsehood of deities in different forms of one way or another. Those who create the absolute falsehood of deities has its roots in total unbelief. This unbelief can extend to an invention of thought in believing in God in general and some of this belief system may make the truth of the existence of the true God obscure or tainted in its doctrines.

Here I will now quote "The Immeasurable" By J. Krishnamurti and his question: "Is God an Invention of Thought?" Here I will Quote his documentation:

"What is religion? Man has sought something that is not of this world. From the most ancient of people till now man has sought something that time, thought, has nothing to do with that. He has sought it. And in his search, he has been trapped by the priests. Priests of the world who become the interpreters of that --- we know, you don't, we will tell you all about it. And the established religions are just nonsense, as far as --- please don't accept this. " For the speaker, they are just entertainment, excitement, the thing to do for a while. If you are young you avoid all that nonsense. As you grow older you get frightened, you become this or that. And all things that are in the churches, temples, and mosques are put together by thought.

God is an invention of thought. So, if we can scrap all that from our brain, from our belief, from our hope, then we are free to enquire what is religion. Etymologically that word has not an exact beginning, it is not " to bind " as was originally thought. So, we are enquiring into what is the religious mind. Not the believing mind that is very simple, very easy to explain. But the religious mind, because the religious mind alone can create a new culture; not the believing mind, not the mind that has faith. So, we are going to enquire into it, if you are not tired.

To enquire into it very deeply one must ask what is meditation. Not how to meditate, not what are the systems of meditation, whether Eastern, Far Eastern, Near East or the present gurus (With their- whether gurus from India or gurus from America, they have got systems, methods, which have all become money making concern. It has no depth to it.) So, if you can abolish all that, put aside all that. That means you are free from all authority to enquire what is meditation. To go into it one must be, as we said, be free from fear, pleasure. The ending of sorrow is the beginning of meditation.

J. Krishnamurti
Public Talk 2, New York, 1983.

PLEASE SHARE YOUR THOUGHTS

The Immeasurable is dedicated to exploring the essential questions of our existence: who we are and where we are going. The intent is to inspire readers to question assumptions of the mind, offering opportunities to ask deep questions into common life themes which are superficially accepted. We encourage an investigation into the fabric of reality and our physical and cultural conditioning. In this exploration, we might find a new understanding of time and its relation to our thinking processes. A perception of the interconnectedness within the totality of life might arise in us as our perception expands through these explorations.

Share your thoughts in the comments below.
Here I have a problem with his denial "that time, thought, has nothing to do with that." Time has everything to do with it; since God is the proprietor of time and that the beliefs that those who place their faith in a God that describes and reveals prophetic events that are related or coincide with world events are well fit in mind and spirit. Some or most here deny what they see and what is obvious in our world that is now and has been down the centuries filled with hatred, violence, sexual perversion, terrorism, deceit, conflict, disease, and poverty. And this is also because of sloth or unemployment because of an overpopulated planet and the deception of religious apostasy in many religions worldwide and in these last days it has been so bad that people fall into depression and anxiety and some people because of their poverty resort to conflict and violence has it is mentioned in 2nd Timothy 3: 1, 2, 3, 4, 5.

Also etymology is the history of linguistic form (as a word) shown by tracing its development since its earliest recorded occurrence in the language where it is found, by tracing its transmission from one language to another, by analyzing it into its component parts, by identifying its cognates in other languages or by tracing it and its cognates to a common ancestral form in an ancestral language. Here Cognates refers to the birth of a word that is derived from an original word or language that formed in early development of that word or language. Here etymology is used as a tool to seek out the truth in ancient writings of language to better help interpret the Biblical records of the Authorized King James Version Bible.

When J. Krishnamurti mentions that it is not the simple mind that is religious. Here J. Krishnamurti is saying only that it is a believing simple mind that believes in the things of this world and not in the things of the God of the Authorized King James Version Bible. And that he is only referring perhaps to believing in intense secularism. Here nothing can be further from the truth since simplicity is connected to the foolish things of this world which is according to being a true believer in God and the Authorized King James Version Bible as it is mentioned in 1st Corinthians 1: 27. Here the Strong's Exhaustive Concordance of the Bible in # 3474 and in # 3473 refers to the term "foolish" as "dull" or "stupid" or "absurd" or "blockhead" or "heedless" or "silly talk" or "buffoonery" or "foolish talking." Here this mention of foolishness is the description of a servant of God as a person who is not part of the world but is close to God according to being severely criticized as a dumb and foolish person who believes in God as J. Krishnamurti explains in his documentation which he has written or has written this short thesis or hypothesis which is considered wise in this world according to being like a scribe who was like the Pharisees who crucified Christ according to 1st Corinthians 1: 19, 20, 21, 22, 23, 24, 25.

Here J. Krishnamurti refers to fear, pleasure as something one must be free from. Fear that the Authorized King James Version Bible speaks of is to not put your trust in man or to fear man or envy sinners (according to Jeremiah 17: 5 and Proverbs 29: 25 and Proverbs 23: 17 and Isaiah 29: 13) who take pleasure in sinning since the pleasure that J. Krishnamurti speaks of refers to those religious apostate Christians who take great pleasure in their sins like having or committing sexual immorality by having more than one wife unlike David who was a just man in the sight of the Lord and that there was a reason for David to have all these wives since he used discretion in the sight of the Lord. And David did not have that amount of wives according to 1st Chronicles 14: 3, 4 and not like his son Solomon who had done evil in the sight of the Lord by having more than a thousand wives as mentioned in the Old Testament according to 1st Kings 11: 1, 2, 3, 4, 5, 6. And also to accumulate riches in excess as Solomon had done according to 2nd Chronicles 9: 22, 23, 24, 25, 26, 27, 28, 29, 30, 31 and here Solomon had corrupted himself by these riches according to 1st Kings 11: 4, 5, 6.

Apostate Christians tend to deny or misunderstand the scriptures as to why we should not have more than one wife --- since in the Old Testament there was a reason for David to have more than one wife. So because of his true faith in God and having that reverential fear towards God and be blessed and instead being cursed by having a fear towards man instead of God where his heart would have departed from God according to Jeremiah 17: 5. That here because of David's strong faith in God is that God had bestowed him with more than one wife. But David's son Solomon had corrupted himself in the end by having all those riches in the sight of the Lord thinking God had blessed him in the end and therefore took advantage of God through a heart that became hardened through deceit or deceiving himself in the end by departing from his faith in God according to Hebrews 3: 12, 13.

The terms "Jesus Freak" or "Religion" or "Religious" or "Bible Thumper" are terms used today and in the past by people who are out right rejectors of the Bible and are secular in nature. Here the Apostle Paul said something about the Biblical definition of religion in his writing to the Romans: "Be not conformed to this world." James tells us that true religion is a devotion to God demonstrated by love and compassion for fellowmen and to visit the fatherless and widows in their affliction and be not coupled with worldliness and to reject those secular desires of this world according to Romans 12: 2 and James 1: 27.

There are also those who are rejectors of the Bible who may deny the truth when they know the truth and see it right in front of them having that nature of misoneism where they plow ahead in sin and iniquity and sow wickedness according to Job 4: 7, 8, 9 and the wicked shall fall by their own wickedness according to Proverbs 11: 5. Also there is the wicked that will or may turn to God in the end according to what the word of God says would happen to a wicked person who practices and has wickedness in his heart and turns from it as the word of God says. And that it is possible for the wicked to reject a wicked mindset and accept the word of God according to Ezekiel 33: 14, 15, 16. Likewise if a righteous person turns to wickedness, then all his righteousness shall not be remembered according to Ezekiel 33: 12, 13.

Religion is a broad term that it is a stereotypical description of either being righteous or wicked. These two terms are misunderstood --- for you can be considered righteous in a secular sense and you could be considered righteous in a sense of rejecting the secular desires of this life. Likewise you can be wicked in a secular sense where you are prone to criminal activity and deceit and end up either dead or incarcerated for a long period of time or for life after committing this criminal activity and deceit according to Proverbs 21: 24, 25 and proverbs 11: 17, 18, 19, 20, 21. Also you can be wicked having a wicked mindset where you turn from a wicked mindset and you reject the desires of a secular life and accept the word of God and live according to Ezekiel 33: 14, 15, 16. Those who have a degree of righteousness in a secular sense tend to reject the prophetic revelations of the Authorized King James Version Bible and the historical evidence of Biblical archaeology but have a form of religious apostasy according to Titus 1: 14, 15, 16 and 2nd Corinthians 11: 13, 14, 15.

Is Religion and Theology different from Biblical studies? Here Religion and Theology is the study of God while Biblical studies is the study of the Bible itself. When you study the Bible each person who studies it has either a different opinion of someone else who has also studied the Bible or has the same opinion of a person who has also studied the Bible. Here they may use the lens of Biblical studies; since they will study the Bible book by book and come up with an interpretation that may be influenced by secularism or a secular life style they have where they deny the faith to fast or deny the prophetic word of God of the end times and the second coming of Christ and believing in false Christ's according to saying to eat and drink for tomorrow we die. Saying that Christ may not come or will delay his second coming etc. according to 1st Corinthians 15: 30, 31, 32, 33, 34 and Matthew 24: 23, 24, and Matthew 24: 48, 49, 50.

Theology itself takes more of a topical approach. It divides the Bible into common themes or categories to better understand the overall message. Although we can able to differentiate the two terms like Theology and Biblical Studies according to Dr. Tiberius Rata, Associate Dean of School of Ministry Studies at Grace, there is often an overlap that occurs. "Whenever we study any book of the Bible, it is both a Biblical and a Theological study because in the process we learn about God, about humanity and about God's creation and rule over His creation" says Rata. God also gave man rule over all the earth and had given him dominion over every living thing according to Genesis 1: 26, 27, 28.

Man had taken this privilege of having dominion over every living thing on the earth that God had given him and brought more of a predatory character to his reign when it began to affect their own kind of when the first murder of Abel by his brother Cain had taken place according to Genesis 4. 1, 2, 3, 4, 5, 6, 8.

This is how violence began on earth and how greed entered the thought of man. Here Biblical studies tend to convince a person that reads the Bible on their own to have their own choice to believe what the Bible actually says, unlike theology that comes from learning off the writings of many people who either share common beliefs of different beliefs of the Bible. Take for instance the different translations of many Biblical texts. We a have a multitude of Bibles and books and a diversity of different religions on this earth that it boggles the mind and that many different cultures of many different people tend to change the meaning of God by the many different religions and Bibles that we have in their translations.

Here the truth has been distorted about who God really is. The Authorized King James Version Bible has a warning about these different religions and that has these many different Biblical translations of how they have added words to the scriptures or has taken words away from these scriptures in these many different translations of the Authorized King James Version Bible as mentioned in and according to Revelation 22: 18, 19.

Furthermore, about a book called "Urantia". Here they declare of what the word "Urantia" means which is the name by which our world or planet is known in the universes. What does the book say about life after death? The authors of the book give a detailed and thrilling account of our progressive journey as we travel through higher levels of existence, a journey that causes us to grow spiritually and intellectually as we pursue our own inner perfection.

Our own inner perfection? We are not perfect until we reach that point of immortality as offered by Christ and his blood that was shed on the cross for our sins and have accepted him by drinking that blood and water to receive the Holy Spirit and eventually where the resurrection into immortality takes place according to John 6: 53, 54, 55, 56, 57, 58, 59, 60, 61, 62, 63, and 1st Timothy 6: 14, 15, 16 and 1st Corinthians 15: 50 , 51, 52, 53, 54, 55. His blood that was shed on the cross for our sins is the remedy to eternal life that makes us immortal and sinless. We are presently sinners and in no way do we have a journey that causes us to grow spiritually and intellectually as we pursue our own inner perfection. We cannot purse our own inner perfection as long as we reject the prophetic revelations of the Authorized King James Version Bible and the path determined by God through the sacrifice and redemption of the blood of Christ that was shed for us all as a price paid for our sins. Our sin brings death when we are prone to temptation that leads to err as we are tempted by lust. And when lust has conceived it bring forth sin and sin when it is finished brings forth death according to James 1: 13, 14, 15, 16, and Galatians 6: 7, 8.

What is unique about this book "Urantia" and its teachings they say? They say that there are several sections that could be considered unique, either as entirely new concepts or as innovative approaches to existing knowledge. Probably the most unique or new concept is on an aspect of deity called "God the Supreme." This is an aspect of God which is actually evolving as all experiential beings, such as ourselves, are evolving to perfection. Every action, thought, and decision that has spiritual value actually contributes to the evolving of God the Supreme. What is significant about this is that it will take the entire family of humankind, on this world and others, to bring the completion of God the Supreme to fruition. With this realization we can find great meaning in our actions in this life and we are encouraged to do our part in serving others and empowering them spiritually.

Evolving to perfection? That is totally absurd to say the least for if this was the case then the world would not have a Bible and our world would be at total peace. But now there is Religious Apostasy and controversy and extreme violence like we have witnessed in not only in school shootings and mall shootings and shootings that have taken place everywhere on this planet --- but the violent atrocities of the war in Israel and the war in

Ukraine since in these last days before Christ comes back that these are mentioned in the Authorized King James Version Bible as perilous times according 2nd Timothy 3: 1, 2, 3, 4, 5, 6, 7, 8, 9.

Here the world would not have a Bible? But there would be some other divine book. Since the Authorized King James Version Bible was given to man by God as a warning manual to life because of the evil in this world and not because of the perfection that this "Urantia Book" is indirectly claiming that our world has. Sexual immorality and violence and deceit like the deceit that this "Urantia Book" is committing to those who are not well informed of the Bible or who are misled or have been deviated away from the truth of Jesus Christ's words and the word of God.

And this book claims the "aspect of deity" called "God the Supreme" and claiming that this aspect of God is actually evolving as experiential beings as ourselves are evolving to perfection and claiming that we can become like gods. This is nothing, but further from the truth since Satan is the "god" of this world with a small "g" and that the excellency of the power of the God of the Authorized King James Version Bible may be of God and not of us like some mere human being that is being trapped in sin and prone to sin and in need of salvation from this sin that has infiltrated this planet with death and destruction where God uses man's sin to destroy himself and the kingdoms or the nations of this earth with the weapons of war according to Jeremiah 51: 20, 21, 22, 23, 24, --- since man desires to be the "god" of this world in numbers and rejecting our Lord and saviour Jesus Christ of the Authorized King James Version Bible according to 2nd Corinthians 4: 4, 5, 6, 7.

And where we should renounce the hidden things of dishonesty and not handling the word of God deceitfully like the authors of "The Urantia Book" have seriously done neglecting the obvious problems that this world has and that man cannot save himself as this Urantia Book claims that man can do. As God asks us to renounce this kind of dangerous thinking and deceit according to 2nd Corinthians 4: 1, 2, 3.

Another new concept described in "The Urantia Book" is that of the thought adjuster, a spirit fragment of God that indwells the mind. Although most religions speak of the inner presence of God, "The Urantia Book" goes into great detail about this part of God that is bestowed on human beings. The thought adjuster is what allows God to maintain close contact and provide spiritual guidance to human beings.

Also are included are advanced teachings on the nature of deity, the Trinity, and previously unrevealed view of the physical structure of the universe in which we live. The Urantia Book also talks about reality on the cosmic level of progression. There is information in "The Urantia Book" that has not been previously revealed, such as God's attributes and personality and our Creator's potential ascension plan for human beings. We are helped to understand the purpose of our existence and why our understanding can be so limited, a perspective that often contributes to our notion that life seems unfair. This can free up one's thinking and elevate the individual to a superconscious level where there may begin the recognition of the light of truth and of beauty and goodness. A challenging and rewarding reading experience is available for adventure seekers who can discover an enlarged way of living and loving.

Does "The Urantia Book" comment on the conditions of the world we live in? Absolutely! There is timely information on the problems of our largely, materialistic society and ways that solutions can be approached. The book's authors examine the reasons for the fragmentation that exists in our religious institutions and delineate the steps necessary to achieve world unity.

What does "The Urantia Book" say about the presence of evil in the world? Evil is described as a choice that is made by the free will of the mortals on the planet. The "Urantia Book" describes two key setbacks in our planetary history, leadership defaults that explain much of the disorder that we see in the world today we call evil. These two events are referred to in the book as the "Lucifer rebellion" as well as the "default" of this world's "Material Son and Daughter," Adam and Eve (though not described in the book as the world's first two human beings). According to "The Urantia Book", despite these two damaging planetary events, individual human beings still enjoy all the avenues available to a normally developing planet for spiritual advancement.

Here a normally developing planet has been nothing but violence and conflict ever since the time of Adam and Eve dating back to Genesis according to Genesis 4: 8 and Genesis 6: 5. Here sin entered the world and man had possessed the Babylonian lifestyle of excessive sex and excessive food and excessive materialism and man had become arrogant by being obsessed with money by deceitful business ventures. Here scams have infiltrated our online life presence and being victims of these online scams. Here Scammers stole an estimated U.S. 1.02 trillion dollars and the countries worldwide with the codes "S" (S$ 1.4 trillion) globally. And also, Singapore victims who lost the most money on average. This was way higher than the US$55.3 billion dollars lost for the whole of 2021 and the US$ 47.8 billion dollars lost in 2020, according to a joint study by non-profit organizations Global Anti-Scam Alliance (Gasa) and data service provider Scam Advisor. The latest figure was revealed by Gasa managing director Jorij Abraham during his opening speech at the Global Anti-Scam Summit in Lisbon, Portugal at an annual conference. The global sum lost to scams was estimated by surveying 49, 459 individuals from 43 countries, including Singapore. Participants were asked about the types of scams they encountered and the amount of money they lost to fraudsters, among other questions. The data was then extrapolated based on the country's population.

The "Urantia Book" mentions the effort man is trying to make with world unity which is another setback because there are more people interested in money than in the Barter System that can be implemented worldwide. So, money will be the cause of division and conflict and war that will lead to destruction and not of unity and peace. This money will developed into a digital format in the next 15 to 20 years by the Mark of the Beast or know as one world digital currency where the world will try to unite under some economic and religious and government social order perhaps by an authoritarian system to compel the world to unite under a shroud filled world of sinners that we all are as mentioned in Revelation 18: 2, 3, 4 and Revelation 17: 12, 13 and Revelation 13: 14, 15, 16, 17, 18 and Romans 3: 23.

Here a Babylonian Religious apostasy will arise and giving way to a world leader known as an Antichrist or Beast who will unite this world of sinners leading to worldwide genocide of true Christians and their converts resulting in Armageddon in the end according to Revelation 20: 4 and

Revelation 6: 9, 10, 11 and 2nd Thessalonians 2: 3, 4 and Revelation 16: 12, 13, 14, 15, 16.

CHAPTER 3
What is Babylon?

Revelation 14 tells how John the divine heard an angel declare that Babylon would be destroyed see Revelation 14: 8. Revelation 16: 19 which begins the account of that destruction, and Revelation chapters 17 and 18 continues the account in greater detail. As in other parts of Revelation, the destruction of Babylon is described using symbolic language. Babylon was the capital city of ancient Babylonia, but in the scriptures the name often referred to the whole nation. In the Old Testament we read that the Babylonians conquered the Kingdom of Judah, taking many Israelites captive to Babylon. The city of Babylon was very large and the people of the city were very wealthy, displaying their riches with fancy buildings, clothing, and leisure activities. They also worshipped idols. Because of the worldliness of Babylon and because it was a place where the children of Israel were captive, the Lord often used the name Babylon in the scriptures to represent sin, worldliness, the influence of the devil on the earth and the spiritual captivity that comes from these things according to Revelation 12: 12. And captivity is often mentioned in the Authorized King James Version Bible but I will mention an example of that here according to Jeremiah 30: 10, 18. Here Babylon is the opposite of Zion as are its values since being Babylonian and having the Babylonian lifestyle of excessive sex and excessive food and excessive materialism definitely makes them not the outcasts of Zion according to Jeremiah 30: 17.

While we've described some history about the sins of this demonic realm's influence over the nations on the earth, it's time to differentiate political and religious power within the human perspective. Mystery Babylon the Great is a symbol in the Book of Revelation that depicts the depraved state of earthly leaders obsessed with secularism. Do we think empires, kingdoms, or cities get weaker as time goes on, or is it the same system in operation with new clothes? There have been many iterations or the recurrence of the evil realm that have interacted closely with human rulers. The relationship will amplify towards the end of this age. This is shown through symbology in the book of Revelation. Here, Babylon is described figuratively to mean all self-centered governments, businesses and religions on the globe.

Bible commentators have thought that Mystery Babylon (Revelation 17: 5) is Rome, Jerusalem, or a restoration of ancient Babylon. Many interpretations have been derived from a vague passage by an angel describing the prostitute in Revelation 17: 18. The woman that you saw is that great city that has dominion over the kings of the earth. The Prostitute is also called Mystery Babylon, or Babylon the Great. The angel does not provide a complete answer in this short verse, so we need to know what the biblical definition of "city" is. Is there a literal city with powerful people working behind the scenes to control rulers over the earth, or is the city symbolic? We will focus our attention on the symbolic.

Throughout history, we noticed that many kings and other leaders had unnatural desires to expand control, wealth and land regions. It seems that they were never satisfied. This hunger for more power is an important aspect to consider in Genesis 6: 1, 2, 3, 4 and Genesis 10: 8, 9, 10, 11, 12, These passages describe the rise of the city state system before and after the flood. The practices of taking multiple wives or building towers are not necessary like they were long ago, yet the desire for control of territories and people remains.

Scripture records that pagan nations heavily influenced Israel to subscribe to the city- state system according to 1st Kings 14: 22, 23, 24 and 2nd Kings 17: 7, 8, 9, 10, 11, 12 and Isaiah 57: 3, 4, 5, 6, 7, 8 ,9, 10. These examples of these scriptures or passages have showed the worship of false gods (with a small "g") described as demons in Deuteronomy 32: 17. We may think that the demonic realm only affected religious practices, but we know the political sphere was integrated with religion through priests and kings. There is a wide range of historical records with priest-kings in Sumer, Egypt, Greece and Rome.

Looking forward, there are only two conclusive cities during the last days of this age and the beginning of the next age according to Scripture. One is the city that God builds as everlasting according to Revelation 21: 1, 2, 3, 4, 5, 6, 7 while the other city is the city that humanity builds, only to be destroyed toward the end of this age. Obviously, Mystery Babylon is the symbolic city that man builds, since there are no good qualities of this woman who rides this Beast One World Government of the Antichrist or Beast or one world Government leader where man in vain tries to save the world from corruption when corruption is present itself in this symbolic city that man organizes and builds the religious and economic and political infrastructure that represents the whole or all world governments on planet earth. Here there are no good qualities of the woman who rides this Beast of a One World Government according to Revelation Chapter 17 or any righteous characteristics found in Revelation Chapter 18.

We know Christ went to "prepare a place" for us mentioned in John 14: 3. We also know this is a dwelling place that man will not build from Nathan's prophecy in 1st Chronicles 17 : 9, 10. There is no human effort achievable to build anything of lasting value when compared to what only God can build for us.

We will see this city called the "New Jerusalem" in the future based upon the vision of Revelation 21: 2, 3, 4. It is designed and built by God with the most wonderful depictions mentioned later in Revelation Chapter 21. The intent was always been for God to dwell with man using His means, not for people to build their own type of system to please him according Acts 17: 22, 23, 24, 25, or to honor themselves. The bad news is that humanity has continually asked for help through alternative means from the demonic, whether knowingly or unknowingly.

The figurative city symbolically known as Babylon that man has constructed over thousands of years is that it developed into and started with the fall of man in Genesis. This concept started with a literal city built by Cain according to Genesis 4: 17. Which was the first civilization, which perished in the Judgment of the Flood, was Cainite in origin, character and destiny. And this concept slowly grew into a bigger concept of corruption after the Flood. The origin birth of this city brought the beginning of corruption to planet earth down through the millenniums and centuries and that the thousands of these years of corruption that have originated from ancient history are to be undone by the 1,000-year kingdom of Christ. And this coming kingdom ruled by Christ will take away the short reign and short lived kingdom of corruption brought on by a ruler known as the Antichrist or Beast of Revelation 17: 12, 13 and the Kingdom of this Beast or Antichrist will be taken by the saints of the most high and Christ which is God according to Revelation 17: 14, Daniel 7: 22, 23, 24, 25, 26, 27 and Revelation 20: 4.

Today we have a world filled with a state of confusion so bad that man has not recognized that the problems are not judicial, political, or religious, or economic but that man himself is being blinded that man believes that he can save himself without the help and guidance from the God of the Authorized King James Version Bible. As I have mentioned in the "INTRODUCTION" segment of this book that Babylon is known for nothing but confusion that has led to immorality and rejection of all things of the divinity of prophetic revelations and presence and existence of the God of the Authorized King James Version Bible.

Here this war in Ukraine and Israel may be all propaganda to elect a world leader to rule with a rod of iron in order solve these world issues like inflation and the economic and political and violent conflicts around the world and the criminal acts of civilians all around the world and the pestilences plaguing humanity like Covid 19. And of this morass we are sinking in and this is all because in the United States which has already spent some 111 billion dollars defending Ukraine. President Joe Biden is advocating for an additional 50 billion dollars in aid which is propaganda to elect a world leader for this one world government know as this Babylonian apostate religious and world economic Empire. But Republican lawmakers are acting like they have no money and balking at more support just like some lawmakers in Europe are on the fence about providing another 50 billion dollars to Ukraine, after failing to deliver on promised ammunition.

The reason the Ukrainians are gloomy is that, they now sense, not only have they not done well this past year of 2023 - to beginning of 2024, but they know that Russians' game is improving as said by Richard Barrons, a former British army general. "They see what's happening in Congress, and they see what happened in the EU." Ukraine may be on the defensive this winter in 2023-24, but its military leaders say they have no intention of letting up the fight. If we won't have a single bullet, we will kill them with shovels, said Serhii, a commander in the 59th Brigade that is active in the eastern city of Avdiivka and who spoke on condition that only his first name be used. "Surely, everyone is tired of war, physically and mentally. But imagine if we stop --- what happens next?"

Here this war may be absolute propaganda that it will get to the point that Donald Trump will be elected as U.S president again where he may convince

Putin to stop the war in Ukraine where Vladimir Putin will make political concessions to the world as a form of deception to form a One World Government with other dictators in the world with the aid of a perhaps coming again U.S. president like Donald Trump where they all eliminate a democratic influence on the world and promising a better world of prosperity and peace on account of a world that has been compelled to conform because of the negative political and economic implications like the burden of excessive and out of control inflation and the deaths of soldiers and civilians and genocidal deaths of all these people caused by the wars in Ukraine and Israel causing to frighten the world into submission to conform to a One World Government of the Beast or Antichrist as mentioned in the Authorized King James Version Bible according to Revelation 17: 12, 13.

These wars in Ukraine and Israel are complete and utter propaganda in order to frighten and compel the world to submit to Donald Trump and elect him for the eventual presidency of the United States and his strategic approach to solve these world political conflicts worldwide. And these economic issues that world is facing now like this out of control inflation and the increase demand for commodities and the unemployment issues and the pestilences plaguing humanity now like a variant of diseases and viruses like Covid 19 and just recently on January 28th / 2024 as mentioned in the news that in the U.K. that there has been an outbreak of the measles. And this measle virus is now spreading at an alarming rate according to Luke 21: 8, 9, 10, 11.

Here this confusion starts within the last few years as troubling for a coming tyrannical One World Government since Vladimir Putin's possible reasons to invade Ukraine was more than a coincidence where here is that this invasion took place a year after Trump lost the election in November / 2020 and after that January 6th / 2021 insurrection that did not have Trump reinstated to the white house but made him out to be a bad political figure like Putin has been all along for his conduct as a president of Russia or being involved in terrorist activity. Here this war in Ukraine was a conspiracy to cause upheaval in the world. Making the world unstable economically and politically in order to have Trump have a very positive consensus to be elected once again to the White House. Here this war in Ukraine and Israel was propaganda at the expense of many, many, lives to place Donald Trump back in the presidential office since violence was perpetrated in the midst of Vladimir Putin and Trump's close relationship with Putin according to Ezekiel 28: 16. Since the relationship Trump has with Putin and other authoritarian figures around the world would end the wars in Ukraine and Israel if Trump was elected once again in the White House. Bringing on that world unity and an emerging tyrannical one world government ruled by perhaps Putin and / or Trump along with other 10 global dictators from around the globe according to Revelation 17: 12, 13.

Here these dictators will take advantage of a planet and that they claim is over populating since the population in the U.S. grew to 335 million people in 2023. Here their purpose would be to claim that the world is in need of a one world government that can govern with an iron fist or claim that the Bible says that this world needs to govern with a rod of iron according Revelation 2: 21, 22, 23, 24, 25, 26, 27. And avoid abortion according to Revelation 2: 22, 23. But here this is the deception of the Antichrist or Beast to use the Bible as a book of morals for their coming One World Tyrannical Government to deceive the populace of the world into accepting their Babylonian materialistic and sexually and monetarily obsessed apostate religious and economic and politically corrupt system order under the rule of an Babylonian worldwide empire according to Revelation chapters 17 and 18.

Here the lack of housing because of the increase of our out of control breeding in our population has now emerged with the population in the U.S. that grew to 335 million people. Here the demand for commodities to feed and house a population that is increasing day by day and out of control leading to housing shortages and sky rocket housing prices and increasing property tax and inflation on food and commodities. Where also food shortages and the lack of a sufficient supply of grain for the world on account of the war in Ukraine and in Israel, has compelled the world to submit to an authoritarian government in each and every country worldwide. And be compelled to forsake a democratic system of governance in each and every country worldwide. Where a Babylonian empire under the rule and dictatorship of a tyrannical dictator emerges in a cunning and deceptive way to give a false message of coming peace to the world and will have a lasting peace worldwide and will not fall into chaos and conflict? But here instead this Babylonian empire will be chaotic and fall into chaos and sudden destruction that will come upon the world because of this deception, according to 1st Thessalonians 5: 1, 2, 3 and Revelation 13: 14, 15, 16 and Revelation 20: 4 and Revelation 6: 9, 10, 11 and Jeremiah 51: 49.

Here as I have mentioned in my other books that no prophecy of the scripture is of any private interpretation according to 2nd Peter 1: 20. So Trump may be just another political figure in our world and perhaps not considered to be the coming Antichrist or Beast as I have kept an open mind here on these implications of Biblical prophecy. Here this war in Ukraine and this other war in Israel may be propaganda to make it appear that Donald Trump is the one who solves these world problems and conflicts and war atrocities that are now taking place at the time of this writing on January 29th / 2024. And therefore, Trump will get elected because of his good standing relationship with Vladimir Putin and with other dictators around the world and with other terrorist organizations worldwide where Donald Trump, if he takes the White House again will be considered a political hero for solving these middle east crises and the war in Ukraine. He will have a boasting heart after this success and claim to be Jesus Christ or God deceiving the whole world who will accept him as this saviour to the world but will not be able to govern 8 billion people because of his sin. And Artificial Intelligence will not help either because is developed by people who have sin and has deceptive features of this Intelligence known as Artificial. Since no man who is a mortal and that has been born in sin on planet earth can take the office or world leadership or takes the place of Christ to rule this planet according to Psalms 24: 1, 2, 3. And because of man's sin no man who is subject to inheriting sin like the rest of us comes short of the glory of God according to Romans 3: 23. And therefore Donald Trump who may become this world leader and saviour will lead the world down a path to temporary peace that will eventually lead to the perdition of civilization of planet earth according to 2nd Thessalonians 2: 3, 4.

CHAPTER 4
Who is God?

Who is God we say? He is considered an extraterrestrial. And the only ultimate powerful and Almighty entity that the world has ever known in the past going back to the ancient period of Genesis and known also to be the Almighty God in the present as well; and God is also known to never change or never have a variable of circumstances drastically change according to Genesis 17: 1, 2, 3, 4 and Genesis 35: 11, 12 and Malachi 3: 6 and James 1: 17.

These extraterrestrial entities work with our God in divine matters in guiding and warning mankind in his negative destiny of things. Where man does not only sin through greed and lust but has a tendency to reject the God of the Authorized King James Version Bible. These extraterrestrial entities are known and have been known down the centuries as "angels" and who work and interact with extraterrestrial beings and carry out the will of God and warn humanity of spiritual and physical impending doom that is about to happen or occur in the near or distant future.

UFO's do exist and are in the pages of the Bible and have known to be a humanoid description as some sort of a creature as mentioned and according to Ezekiel 1: 4, 5, 6. Here UFOs and aliens are mythically to be known as little green men from Mars or outer space etc. And angels have been known to have halos on their heads and wings on their bodies. These descriptions are the results of ancient witness accounts of beings that appeared to man as extraterrestrial angels that were floating apparitions that appeared to men in ancient times to warn man in a spiritual or physical way and / or to carry out the work of God. So, these men back thousands of years ago may have claimed that these apparitions of floating beings that appeared to them believed they were actually flying in this floating condition in these visions or divine appearance that these men saw. Therefore, giving the description of these unidentified sightings as beings with wings. And therefore the term "angel" that is mentioned in the Bible was labelled and described as a man that had the wings of a bird since ancient man had this description only as having a being described has having wings and using the subject and description of bird's wings to describe these angels that appeared to them as being men and with having birds' wings on their backs. Not only did Angels appear as a flying apparition as beings flying but as an army to smote the enemies of God and also known to have the presence of a flame or burning fire like a bush or having the presence of fire in some other places as in a bush or appearing as being as a flaming minister or for an angel to appear in a dream according to Matthew 1: 20 and Psalms 104: 3, 4 and 2nd Kings 19: 34, 35 and Exodus 3: 2.

Also some of these angels with wings are a mythological legend of angels considered as an apparition from being as innocent and peaceful looking as conjured up by man's imagination having a halo with wings on their backs and dwelling in fluffy white clouds above the earth that represents heaven -- but in reality some apparitions of angels are from the God of the Authorized King James Version Bible and that they have an appearance as a frightening entity like Christ was that appeared to John the Divine on Patmos Island according to Revelation 1: 14, 15, 16, 17, 18 and Judges 6: 22, 23.

Here John the Divine was exiled on a small rocky island in Aegean that is a place where many criminals of Rome were sent there to serve their prison terms under harsh conditions who was also exiled to this island there for preaching the word of God and for our testimony about Jesus Christ. And I John Bazzanella had suffered a related fate which I was also had been burdened by the authorities for preaching the word of God as well and being incarcerated for 40 years in and out of psychiatric institutions when I did not hurt anyone and had no criminal or psychiatric record prior to this crime of ramming this police cruiser and being charged unjustly with attempted murder on a cop for ramming a police cruiser according to Ecclesiastes 5: 8, 9 and Psalms 82: 2.

Who is God? Does Vladimir Putin know who God is? He has committed genocide on the people of Ukraine and then has the audacity to practice his religious faith as a person who possesses a false faith according to 2nd Peter 2: 1, 2, 3, 4, 5, 6, 7, 8, 9, 10, 11, 12, 13, 14, 15.

Although Putin claims to be Russian Orthodox. His mother was a devoted

Christian believer who attended the Russian Orthodox Church, while his father was an atheist. Though his mother kept no icons at home, she attended church regularly, despite government persecution of her religion at that time. Vladimir Putin's mother secretly baptized him as a baby, and she regularly took him to church services. According to Vladimir Putin, his religious awakening began after a serious car crash involving his wife in 1993, and a life-threatening fire that burned down their dacha in August 1996 a dacha is also known as a cottage or second home. Shortly, before an official visit to Israel, Putin's mother gave him his baptismal cross, telling him to get it blessed. Putin states " I did as she said and then put the cross around my neck. I have never taken it off since.

When asked in 2007 whether he believes in God, he responded: "there are things I believe, which should not in my position, at least, be shared with the public at large for everybody's consumption because that would look like self-advertising or a political striptease." Putin's rumoured confessor is Russian Orthodox Tikhon Shevkunov. The sincerity of his Christianity has been rejected by his former advisor Sergi Pugachev.

So, does Putin know who God is? Or is he a goat as the Bible symbolically speaks of the goat that draws a distinction for the term sheep. Since this distinction between these two livestock especially in a parable that we will discuss later in this chapter are different but at the same time cunningly similar in appearance.

So, what actually is different from a goat to a sheep? Apart from the fact that they look cunningly similar they are actually different; the characteristics of these animals may hint at the reasons why believers are sheep and unbelievers and / or apostate Christians are goats.

Sheep are dependent on their shepherd. They have a reputation for not topping the lists of the most intelligent animals, but they do trust and depend on their shepherd. Goats on the other hand have a reputation for self- reliance and stubbornness. This could, perhaps, reflect the worldly idea of leaning on one's self for support and guidance rather than God.

Here goats have destructive tendencies. Here Shepherds are known to protect sheep from their environment, whereas goatherds protect the environment from their goats since they are known to be more destructive and dangerous and more violent than sheep are. Goats and sheep are hard to tell apart unless you get a good look at them. Here Putin at one time was thought to have been a good Russian Leader but now after telling him apart from the true Christians that are known as sheep, Putin was found out to be just recently a goat instead, and just recently was found out to be completely violent and seriously destructive towards humanity on a very large scale by these two wars that have erupted in Ukraine and Israel. And the problems that these two wars have caused like the political and economic issues that have arisen in our world's economy and political spectrum. That possessed out of control diplomatic problems for democratic leaders in each and every democratic country worldwide where world war is imminent. And the prospect of out of control inflation worldwide that is becoming a threat to world peace, or whatever is left of world peace.

In the end or in the consummation of this age we will finally and really find out who God is? And the Nations will see that the true sheep are not only the true followers of Christ but will rule with him since they will be morally fit to govern and not like Vladimir Putin or Donald Trump who is mentioned on CNN News as politicians who are not fit to rule and wanting to eliminate democracy as a whole. So how can we tell the Goats from the Sheep? Here Christ at his coming will take all those who have accepted the Mark of the Beast or Global citizenship I.D. who were faithful and loyal to the Beast or Antichrist or swore allegiance to this World Leader or Dictator known as the Beast or Antichrist of Revelation 17: 12, 13 and Revelation 13: 14, 15, 16, 17, 18 and cast them out of the Kingdom into outer darkness to be punished or condemned eternally according to Matthew 25: 46. But the righteous centurion who was humble who had authority claimed he was not worthy of Christ according to Matthew 8: 8, 9, 10, 11 and did not have the attitude that Donald Trump or Vladimir Putin have where Donald Trump and Vladimir Putin are as of now being totally arrogant and having a possessive nature believing that God is with them since they are totally secular being the children of the Kingdom of the Antichrist or Beast of Revelation chapters 17 and 18; and sensing and believing to be like the centurion who was faithful to Christ that they are worthy according to Matthew 8: 8, 9, 10, 11 --- that when or if that time comes they will be known as unprofitable servants and be cast out of the kingdom into outer darkness according to Matthew 25: 30 and according to Matthew 8: 12. So these are the Goats and the Sheep as I have mentioned here that the Goats are those who are faithful to the Beast or Antichrist or World Leader and Dictator and will be separated from the Sheep who are faithful to Christ at his coming who these sheep will be blessed and inherit the kingdom of Christ at his coming according to Matthew 25: 31, 32, 33, 34, 35, 36, 37, 38, 39. But the goats will be separated for judgment and a curse according to Matthew 25: 41, 42, 43, 44, 45, 46.

CHAPTER 5
Committing Genocidal Peace

What is committing Genocidal Peace? When a country like Russia Invades a country like Ukraine --- it is about regaining the political position and territory that Russia had lost after the Soviet Union collapsed. Here the excuse that Putin claims of Ukraine taking territory from Russia is Bogus to say the least. Ukraine has fought back courageously against Putin's warped bid to restore territory lost to Moscow with the collapse of the Soviet Union and has continued to defy the odds by defending itself against Russian onslaughts with the help of Western Military aid. Was this invasion propaganda for a bigger world plan or conspiracy by the elite of this world to plan some sort of One World Government to possess the world's economy, Religious institutions in order to forge this One World Government in place? Claiming in the near coming future that a coming U.S. future president like Donald Trump who is friendly to dictatorial leadership regimes around the world would be hailed as a hero for ending the war in Ukraine and the war in Israel. Here Donald Trump would be considered a hero as the world would accept him as a savior to humanity because of protecting the world from a mad dictator named Vladimir Putin. Since in September / 2023 Putin staged a televised address in which he ordered a partial military mobilization of 300,000 reservists and reiterated his threat to use nuclear weapons against the West, a major escalation of his rhetoric in which he assured the world that this threat was not a bluff as he has been quoted as saying that "It's not a bluff."

Here tyrants commit genocidal peace as a form of political, religious, and economic and character ethnic cleansing perpetrated by the elite to bring about their One World Government of Revelation Chapters 17 & 18. Tyrants create Empires. Have you ever heard of a democratic Empire? Here the guise is bringing about peace by genocide and so by peace he shall destroy many or this tyrannical mindset who is Vladimir Putin and the coming U.S. president who may be Donald Trump will destroy many by this genocidal peace according to Daniel 8: 24, 25. But he shall fail in the end without the help or the hand of an adversary who would be against him in whatever war he would be involved in since as Daniel 8: 25 says "But he shall be broken without hand." In other words, tyrannical leaders and their governments usually end up destroying themselves in the end. When in the end these tyrannical attempts at governing will trouble this tyrannical type of governing by tidings or worldwide media reports where false religion and deception leads to severe conflict and all-out war according to Daniel 11: 44. And these tyrants who are involved with this sole supreme tyrant shall come to an end. And according to this leading sole supreme tyrant will come to his end as well and none shall help him who is known as this tyrannical dictator known as the Antichrist or Beast is according Daniel 11: 43, 44, 45 and Revelation 17: 10, 11, 12, 13, 14.

Even now the conspiracy of genocidal peace is taking place like Donald Trump who has said on December 19th / 2023 as revealed in the media that immigrants from psychiatric institutions and prisons are poisoning our country. So, we got to get them out or have them deported. Since I was born in Italy and came to Canada when I was two years old, ---- so was Donald Trump also referring to me?

Here we have corrupt government officials being critical of Israel and the Jews where even a doctor named Yipeng Ge was suspended from his University of Ottawa residency after making social media posts critical of Israel. He also announced his resignation from the Canadian Medical Association board of directors, noting his relationship with the organization had become untenable and irreparable. Then there are a scant few who are masking their faces for other reasons --- such as a small number who have committed vandalism and other illegal acts during rallies. Also, those at a pro-Palestinian event in Toronto at Nathan Phillips Square placed a toy on the ground, in front of City Hall, for every Palestinian and Israeli child killed in the war. The ever-growing death toll has been accompanied by an ever-rising tide of anguish that underlies many of the pro-Palestinian events. Here more than 20,000 Palestinians have been killed, according to the Hamas- controlled health ministry in Gaza. There has been those who have lost entire branches of their families.

Here these atrocities are so bad that the internationally regarded, peer review medical journal "The Lancet found no evidence of inflated mortality reporting from the Gaza Ministry of Health." The horrors of the war in Gaza have left little public space, some say, to grieve the loss of those killed in the original Hamas attack that took place on October 7th / 2023. Vigils for the Israeli hostages have shown their faces on large placards, and featured their loved ones appealing that the men, women and children abducted not be forgotten amid the fighting in Gaza and that the toll and trauma of that event not be allowed to be just swept away. The communities have been grieving, that much is clear. It also fuels what we are seeing in the streets and at commemorations. It has also at times become darker and even more vengeful.

Also, accusations of bigotry are made in all directions. Pro-Israeli groups have called rallies in solidarity with Palestinians "hate marches" and accused them of Supporting Hamas, who they claim calls for the death of Jews. Speakers at these marches take care to loudly proclaim they are anti-Zionist, not antisemitic since a "Zionist" refers to a high-profile Jew who is considered someone who rules for God or is symbolically known as a "high mountain." And at these rallies they are proud to have anti-Zionists Jews in attendance. They do have some chants which are supportive of some Hamas's military actions, including the oft- repeated "When people are occupied, resistance is justified."

Some pro-Palestinians speakers, meanwhile, charge all Zionists with racism. They frequently say the state of Israel is itself racist. Many pro-Israeli organizations chief among them, the Centre for Israel and Jewish Affairs (CIJA), have taken to posting video and imagery submitted to them from pro-Palestinian demonstrations they consider evidence of antisemitism. Centre for Israel and Jewish Affairs (CIJA) has been widely criticized for taking the video snippets they post out of context and ascribing bad faith readings of what is being depicted. In one notable instance, Centre for Israel and Jewish Affairs (CIJA) posted a video that protesting students were saying "Judah" meaning Jew. The video was later deleted after consultation with other students present who maintained they were saying Trudeau. Events have largely been peaceful. Yet they on occasion plat-formed extreme views. Often, the most controversial rhetoric has come from prominent people--- including the organizers behind some of Toronto's largest events. Take the Palestinian Youth Movement (PYM), which has coordinated the largest protests in Toronto.

Two days after Hamas's October 7th / 2023 attack, which killed 1,200 people, mostly civilians, the Palestinian Youth Movement (PYM), made a post to its Facebook page referring to it as "active decolonization of Palestinian land led by the Palestinian resistance... in response to decades of brutal colonization and occupation." It also held rallies across Canada and the United States in the wake of the attack.

Toronto 4 Palestine, another major organizer, was accused of antisemitism in the days after the war began when the group posted a statement on social media that was widely seen to deny, without basis, that Hamas was responsible for the October 7th / 2023 attack and to cast doubt on the Holocaust. Meanwhile David M. Weinberg, the Israel office director of Centre for Israel and Jewish Affairs (CIJA), a Canadian Zionist organization headquarters in North York, Toronto, which has organized major local events, received his own backlash for a post on the social media platform X in Mid- December.

Weinberg wrote disparagingly of international law and said concerns for Palestinian civilians should fall to the wayside as Israel battles Hamas. Toronto police said the rallies themselves have been becoming more antagonistic, with some attendees reportedly using more hateful language, imagery, and even violence. At one anti-Israel rally, an attendee held up a sign replacing the Star of David on the Israeli flag with a swastika. The incident which happened at Yonge-Dundas Square in Toronto was investigated by police but did not lead to charges. Toronto4 Palestinian, the organization that coordinated the event, later distanced themselves from the protestor, and they had asked her to cover the offensive sign.

At a separate event a pro-Israel counter protestor held up an image of a man in a kaffiyeh holding a knife with the text that said, "This is not a victim." He and other counter protestors chanted "Fuck, Fuck Palestine," a corruption of the common refrain "Free, Free Palestine."

The man the Toronto Star confirmed was Meir Weinstein, former head of the Canadian chapter of the Jewish Defense League (JDL), classified as a far-right hate group by the FBI. Weinstein had in recent weeks been calling for Canadian Jews to arm themselves and a digital poster was seen by the Toronto Star advertising the counter protest that contained the slogan "Every Jew a .22." Here Mainstream Jewish and pro-Israel groups have publicly denounced and distanced themselves from Weinstein and that JDL Weinstein has previously likened gay people to Nazis and has partnered with the soldiers of Odin, a far- right Islamophobic group. At a pro-Israel event, Raheel Raza, the founder of the "Council of Muslim Against Antisemitism" was a featured speaker. In a letter opposing her visit to the Minnesota House of Representatives Melissa Hortman called her "an extremist who is associated with anti-Muslim hate groups."

At multiple pro- Palestinian rallies in Toronto and Vancouver based activity Harsha Walia has spoken to crowds about how all " struggles against colonialism are interlinked." At a rally two days after Hamas's deadly incursion into Israel Walia praised aspects of their attack: "Palestinians razed to the ground or destroyed to the ground one of the most potent symbols of oppression and apartheid and colonialism in the world today."
Here it is these voices that have served as ammunition for those who seek to dismiss the more peaceful contingents or the possibility of these local protest movements that may bring a more peaceful solution. In seeing these comments, these blog posts, these speakers, moderates may feel pressured to avoid showing up to events, further whittling away rally attendees to those with only the most hardline views. At a pro-Palestinian protest in downtown Toronto, demonstrators burst into Starbucks location, and yelled at employees and gave them the middle finger. Although it has never been on the long-standing public boycott list for companies that support Israel and its army, the international coffee house chain has become a recent target of pro-Palestinian activists after it criticized its union for a social media post over the Israel- Hamas war.

Other Canadian businesses and public figures that have been frequently targeted include Scotia bank for its investment in controversial Israeli weapons manufacturer Elbit Systems Ltd., and indigo founder Heather Reisman, for her charity that supports ex-soldiers who volunteered to join the Israeli army. Activists say the targeting of specific individuals and companies for specific actions is legitimate and should not be branded as antisemitic.

Here some major Jewish organizations have said the threat being felt by such protests is meant to intimidate Canadian Jews and leaves them all subject to attack. Jewish groups speaking out publicly in support of

Palestinians, meanwhile, have had a hand in planning many of these protests themselves. Critics say the latter groups are much smaller and do not represent mainstream Jewish thought.

Mayor Olivia Chow condemned a protest that targeted one Israeli coffee shop, saying "there is no place in our city for antisemitism, Islamophobia, hate, intimidation or harassment of any kind." Meanwhile, Israel supporters also have a message for companies, public figures and politicians who have not spoken up in their defense and they are taking down names. At a rally in November, Jeff Rosenthal, chair of UJA Federation of greater Toronto, told the crowd this should affect their personal, business, civic and philanthropic relationships "for years to come."

The media is failing. That is at least, the conclusion of those with strong feelings around this conflict. At pro-Israel rallies, speakers have derided most Canadian outlets for not labelling Hamas a terrorist organization, for not devoting enough coverage to rising antisemitism and platforming opinion essays or editorials that have called for a ceasefire. The Toronto Star has noted in stories that Hamas has been designated a terrorist group by Canada and other countries but due to the lack of an international consensus, and like other outlets, has stopped short of calling it a terrorist organization. At a pro-Palestinian protest, organizers have accused Canadian media of pro-Israel bias and of failing to regularly cover their movement and its demand. They criticize the media for not calling the conflict in Gaza a genocide. Again, because the lack of Consensus, the Toronto Star does not describe that conflict as a genocide, but has spoken to and quoted experts and organizations who label it as such. Pro-Palestinian organizers also regularly instruct people who attend their rallies not to speak to journalists, whom they say might look for opportunities to twist their words. But Instead, they make their own trained media spokespeople available. Here the reason we don't have enough of a consensus is because those who fail to submit to a peaceful solution are choosing this criticism of this war by not calling it a genocide but being bias against Israel and the Jewish people and being infidels and not believing in Christ and the Authorized King James Version Bible and being also in numbers as the god of this world with a small "g" according to 2nd Corinthians 4: 4.

Hope and fear, and optimism and cynicism, may be emotions that are diametrically opposed. But for those who have raised their voices on either side of the conflict over the past 11 weeks, and those complex feelings somehow co-exist. Regarding the prospect of a sustainable peaceful solution in the Middle East, there's a sense of pessimism for many, who recognize relations between the Israeli government and the Palestinian authorities are arguably at their lowest point in decades. Others have admitted that they feel as though a two-state solution which countries like Canada have supported, is likely no longer tenable. Mercifully, to many, that has not been enough to stop some in the global community from continuing to push relentlessly for it.

Looking ahead into the short-term, almost everyone who spoke to the Toronto Star expressed hope and a belief that the situation in Gaza and Israel will improve. For many individuals, that unwavering optimism is a way to help cope with the current pall or loss of strength in this optimism and being subjected to this pall of darkness will be inevitable.

Despite being displaced from his home in Gaza City and witnessing death all around him, Canadian Palestinian Mansour Shouman told the Toronto Star that he and those sheltering in the city of Khan Younis still remain hopeful and place their faith in God. That outlook, he says, is what helps them get through each day.

Similarly, Maayan Shavit of Toronto, whose, two relatives were held hostage, remained optimistic even when her family wasn't on the initial list of freed hostages during the truce in November.

I'm over-joyed, I'm so happy, she said crying, when news of the release of the first hostages broke. I'm sorry. I'm over- emotional. I'm also very sad my cousins are not coming home. The fight is not over. It's not over, but it's such a joyful day. Five days later, one of Shavit's two relatives was released. Here they are saying to remain hopeful and place their faith in God. But they may through desperate measures eventually accept a dictator to end the war in Israel and Ukraine where this dictator will bring about a false peace. Here if Christ comes in his Father's name that they may not receive him --- but if another shall come in his own name like perhaps Donald Trump or his successor that here they will receive him or as this scripture says "him ye will receive" according to John 5: 43.

Donald Trump will have influence around the world towards terrorist organizations like Hamas who support Russian president Vladimir Putin and other Dictators around the world. On February 11th / 2024 Trump has said to the media and at his rally that he would encourage Russia to "do whatever the hell they want" to any NATO country that doesn't pay enough like meet spending guidelines on defense. And in a stunning admission he would not abide by the collective defense clause at the heart of the alliance if re-elected. Trump said "NATO was busted until I came along," as Trump said at a rally in Conway, South Carolina. Trumps says "I said, everybody is going to pay." They said, "Well, if we don't pay, are you still going to protect us?" I said, "Absolutely not." They couldn't believe the answer. Trump said "one of the presidents of a big country" at one point asked him whether the US would still defend the country if they were invaded by Russia even if they don't pay. "No, I would not protect you," Trump recalled telling that president. In fact, I would encourage them to do whatever the hell they want. You got to pay. You got to pay your bills.

President Biden has restored our alliances and made us stronger in the world because he knows every commander in chief's first responsibility is to keep the American people safe and hold true to the values that unite us .... Encouraging invasions of our closest allies by murderous regimes is appalling and unhinged --- and it endangers American national security, Global stability, and our economy at home, White House spokesperson Andrew Bates said in a Statement.

NATO Secretary General Jens Stoltenberg said that Trump's comments about the alliance put European and American soldiers at risk. Any Attack on NATO well be met with a united and forceful response," Stoltenberg said in a statement. "Any suggestion that allies will not defend each other undermines all of our security, including that of the U.S. and puts American and European soldiers at increased risk. European Council President Charles Michel described comments from Trump on NATO "reckless," adding they "serve only Putin's interest." Reckless statements on NATO's security and Article 5 solidarity serve only Putin's interest. They do not bring more security or peace to the world," Michel said in a post on X. The Transatlantic Alliance has underpinned the security and the prosperity of

Americans, Canadians and Europeans for 75 years. At the core of the North Atlantic Treaty Organization and enshrined in Article 5 of the treaty is the promise of collective defense --- that an attack on one member nation is an attack on all the nations in the alliance. Trump has long complained about the amount other countries in NATO spend on defense compared with the United States and has repeatedly threatened to withdraw the U.S. from NATO. But his comments are his most direct indication he does not intend to defend NATO allies from Russian attack if he is re-elected. Trump has for years inaccurately described how NATO funding works. NATO has a target that each member country spends a minimum of 2% of gross domestic product on defense, and most countries are not meeting that target. But the figure is a guideline and not a binding contract, nor does it create "bills." Member countries haven't been failing to pay their share of NATO's common budget to run the organization.

Republican Sen. Marco Rubio, who has endorsed Trump, said he had "zero concerns" about the former president's NATO comments. Rubio told CNN's Jake Tapper on the "State of the Union" that Trump was merely reflecting on an anecdote or unpublished items of concern from his presidency arguing member nations weren't "paying their dues" until Trump "used leverage" to push NATO countries to "step up to the plate." Trump's just the first one to express it in these terms." The Florida Republican said.

As president, Trump privately threatened multiple times to withdraw the United States from NATO, according to The New York Times. Trump has described NATO as "obsolete" and has aligned himself with Russian President Vladimir Putin and went as far to side with the Russian leader over the U.S. intelligence community over Russia's interference in the 2016 presidential election.

Here all of these claims made by these political entities is all pure propaganda. Furthermore, on CP-24 news in Toronto on February 15 / 2024 it was mentioned that Putin mentioned that he hopes president Biden will be elected in 2024, this is further propaganda perpetrated by Vladimir Putin. They know what is going on throughout the world with other leaders worldwide. Because if this were not the case then these wars in Ukraine and Israel would spread and get out of control to the point that the conflict would get to the point that Vladimir Putin would end up killing himself and

Donald Trump by maiming this world with nuclear weapons that would affect not only Putin, but his so called American Colleague Donald Trump. Why would Putin let this war in Ukraine get out of control? Why after this invasion of Ukraine and the aid of Hamas trying to wipe out Israel would Putin be suicidal? And then even after --- have the rest of the civilization destroyed by killing off some of the politicians in this conspiracy to rule this world by the dictatorships who want to possess the world to themselves and enslave humanity by computers and Artificial Intelligence? It basically makes no sense period!!

Here they are now also at a point that Hamas's success on the war in Israel has given Hamas an advantage of gaining even more support for more weapons from Hamas supporters in this conflict between Hamas and Israel giving Donald Trump and Vladimir Putin leverage politically. So it is possible that at the time of this writing of February / 2024 that because of the blood shed of these two wars in Israel and in Ukraine that Trump's indictment will receive immunity from prosecution and if not this; then he will get elected in hopes of bringing a peace that the world may hope for and cow to --- by accepting Donald Trump as a saviour to the world that comes in his own name according to John 5: 43, 44 and replacing Christ according to 2nd Thessalonians 2: 3, 4 and Psalms 24: 1, 2, 3, 4.

Here as it says in Jeremiah 15: 21 "And I will deliver thee out of the hand of the wicked, and I will redeem thee out of the hand of the terrible." As it says here that a servant of God is delivered by God from the hand of the wicked and redeemed from the hand of the terrible. Here it is also possible that this servant of God is also chastised in a furnace in a mortal state during this chastisement before he would be resurrected or be redeemed into immortality while being in this burning furnace and during this furnace sentence according to Jeremiah 15: 14.

Who are the "wicked"? Perhaps a multitude of political leaders aiming to assassinate this servant of God who are involved with this one world government of the Antichrist having this servant of God under surveillance for the purpose of assassination through their powerful servants who submit to these evil and "wicked" political entities who are involved with the Antichrist.

Who are the "terrible"? Those, involved with the Antichrist who are barbaric to the point that when the "wicked" fail to assassinate this servant of God that the "terrible" here will eventually try to sentence this servant of God to a furnace to prove to the world in one last ditched effort that he is not a servant of God. Here the term "terrible" according to the Strong's Exhaustive Concordance of the Bible Old Testament # 6184 from # 6206 refers to "fearful" i.e. "powerful or tyrannical" --- "mighty," "oppressor," in "great power" "strong" "terrible" "violent" "to awe" "to dread" "hence to harass" "be affrighted" ("afraid" "dread" "feared" "terrified") "break" "dread" "fear" "oppress" "prevail" "shake terribly."

Here Donald Trump will have influence around the world towards terrorist organizations like Hamas who support Russian president Vladimir Putin and other dictators around the world. Now Gaza has become a ruinous heap. Here "Gaza Sanjak" in Arabic as Bilad Ghazza (the land of Gaza) was a sanjak (or was the administrative divisions of the Ottoman Empire) of the Damascus Eyalet, Ottoman Empire centered in Gaza. Which Gaza also known as a part of Damascus has become today as the "burden of Damascus" that has become a ruinous heap due to this war in Israel that was started by Hamas according to Isaiah 17: 1.

Also, Hamas's success on Israel has given Hamas an advantage of gaining more support for more weapons from Hamas's supporters in this conflict between Hamas and Israel giving Donald Trump and Vladimir Putin leverage politically. And it's also possible at the time of this writing of February 16th / 2024 that because of the blood shed of these two wars of Israel and Ukraine that Trump may receive immunity from prosecution. Why? Because Donald Trump becoming president would be that having Donald Trump in the White House there would be negotiating advantages with Vladimir Putin and Russia in general to end these wars in Israel and Ukraine because of Trump having good relationships with dictators around the world especially with China's leader Xi Jinping.

Here at the time of this writing on February 16th / 2024 there was testimony in court from District Attorney Nathan Wade who is the lead prosecutor for District Attorney Fani Willis who is prosecuting Donald Trump. While presiding over the investigation and prosecution of former President Donald Trump and 18 of his allies for attempting to reverse

Georgia's 2020 presidential election results, Fulton County Georgia, District Attorney Fani Willis has made two severe lapses in judgment --- two too many.

In June 2022 she held a fundraiser for the political opponent of Republican Georgia state Sen. Burt Jones, one of the Trump Allies targeted in her investigation. Willis had announced the investigation over a year earlier in February 2021. The optics are horrific, Fulton County Judge Robert McBurney said about the fundraiser before disqualifying Willis and her staff from pursing charges against Jones in July 2022. (While a separate prosecutor may investigate Jones, who has denied any wrongdoing, no one has yet been selected.)

More recently, Willis admitted to having a "personal relationship" with Nathan Wade, a special prosecutor she hired to help with Trump's prosecution. Her admission came in response to Trump co-defendant Michael Roman's court filing claiming Willis and Wade had a clandestine relationship, seeking to remove them from the case. A hearing is being held on the request to remove Willis as the Prosecutor against Trump for allegedly engaging in an improper romantic relationship that amounted to a conflict of interest. Trump's co- defendants in the case are also trying to get all charges dismissed.

The current evidence in the public domain does not establish that either Willis or Wade committed any crimes or violated their ethical obligations as licensed attorneys. And both lawyers vehemently deny any improprieties. As Wade said in his affidavit, "The District Attorney received no funds or personal financial gain from my position as Special Prosecutor." But if Wade did inflate his bills or if Willis did benefit from any of Wade's earnings, those activities would be unethical if not unlawful. And they could lead to disqualification by the Judge.

"The state has admitted a relationship existed," presiding Judge Scott McAfee said at the hearing. "So, what remains to be proven is the existence and extent of any financial benefit, again if there even was one. Because I think it's possible that the facts alleged by the defendant could result in disqualification." He said the evidentiary hearing would establish the record on those core allegations.

Moreover, even the prospect of this impropriety could allow Trump to assert a defense (in court and in the public square) that the cases against him are part of a pattern of prosecution that amounts to a witch hunt undertaken by a corrupt system.

Finally, and most importantly, Willis and Wade should recuse themselves because these controversies and even the appearance of corruption simply cannot be allowed to reach the jury and infect the trial. This could happen if the judge allows Trump's Attorneys to raise them in court. Or it could happen if the related media coverage reaches jurors outside the courthouse. If even one juror thinks Willis was motivated to prosecute Trump to enrich a romantic partner instead of to do justice, it could switch the verdict from guilty to not guilty. Jury trials often turn on far less.

Fortunately, however, this can still be avoided. If Willis and Wade recuse themselves promptly, this controversy is unlikely to taint the trial. Their continued presence on the case is what drives these concerns. and while the defendants raised controversy with the court, it's actually the prosecution's effort that's harmed by it.

If Willis and Wade step aside, other competent lawyers can make the case that Trump violated the law. A full and robust presentation of evidence could still be presented at trial. And because the Fulton County prosecutorial team is large, including two other special prosecutors already on the case, the recusals wouldn't likely cause the trial to be delayed until after the election. This saga is thus a huge problem with a simple and effective solution.

But here it is also possible that if this trial and the prosecution of Donald Trump and his co-defendants is derailed due to District Attorney Fani Willis's relationship with Special Prosecutor District Attorney Nathan Wade, is that Donald Trump's prosecution and the prosecution of his co-defendants if found guilty would be that this prosecution would be delayed until after the election. And Donald Trump would be able to run as a presidential candidate in the election. And if Donald Trump is elected it would make him possibly immune from prosecution since the clause in the Constitution is not clear or is vague regarding prosecuting a sitting president. And also, his co-defendants would also be immune from prosecution since here if Donald Trump is president is that he would pardon his co-defendants from any prosecution or even have the charges dropped. It is stated in the University of Virginia School of Law that --- does the impeachment clause imply that you cannot prosecute people who are subject to impeachment and you have to wait until you've removed them? For everyone other than the president, everybody agrees that of course you can prosecute them while they're in office --- there's no bar in the Constitution's impeachment clause or elsewhere to prosecuting a sitting secretary of defense or a judge, or a general or an ambassador. The impeachment provisions in the Constitution aren't read to bar prosecutions of these officials while they're still in office. But the Office of Legal Counsel believes that the president is different, and that the impeachment provisions somehow signal in the case of the presidency that you cannot prosecute a sitting president. And of course, the problem with that is there's only one set of impeachment provisions, and they don't say that we treat the president any differently. They don't say that other people can be prosecuted while they're in office, but impeachment is the only means of accountability for the presidency. So, they're reading a set of provisions that are in the Constitution in one way for everyone else and in another way for the president.

Was this Fani Willis and Nathan Wade relationship a deliberate conflict of interest or was this relationship a legitimate conflict of interest that happened or occurred by chance that has given Donald Trump this opportunity to overcome this case that was being or was prosecuted by Fani Willis and Nathan Wade's involvement by leading in prosecuting Donald Trump also and by aiding Fani Willis to prosecute Trump as well ?
 On March 1st / 2024 as mentioned on CNN news Channel that Donald Trump showed up during Fani Willis's disqualification in court who was a prosecuting attorney against Donald Trump. Here Fani Willis surprisingly showed up in court and appearing not burdened. But why would Fani Willis be at ease by this disqualification for being declared by the court to be disqualified as an attorney who was prosecuting Donald Trump and be at ease in front of prominent people and the general public and while being in the media? But is Fani Willis and Nathan Wade against Trump as well or is it a front to have this relationship being done behind our backs deliberately; and deliberately being caught in the act?

And also, here Donald Trump showed up in court as a sign of gratitude towards Fani Willis and Nathan Wade by showing up in court as a gesture of appreciation and gratitude? Was this conspiracy deliberately a planned relationship and being deliberately caught in the act in this relationship that was to get Donald Trump cemented into immunity from prosecution in order to have the prospect of being elected in November / 2024 as president in order to end the wars in Israel and Ukraine? And to avoid a nuclear confrontation with democratic nations in the end? Bringing on this One World Government of the Antichrist or Beast of Revelation 17: 12, 13? If another comes not in Christ's name, him will they receive, according to John 5: 40, 41, 42, 43 ,44.

Was this relationship a deliberate conflict of interest that was a conspiracy that was carefully planned in order to have Donald Trump reach the election in November / 2024 and be a prospect for winning this election cementing him into immunity from prosecution for these allegations and charges against him? Only time will tell now. And so as it goes that this Genocidal Peace has a price and as U.S president Dwight D. Eisenhower has said on April 16th / 1953, "Chance for Peace" : "Every gun that is made, every warship launched, every rocket fired signifies, in the final sense, a theft from those who hunger and are not fed, those who are cold and are not clothed."

Here the world looks for peace and so does Donald Trump and his followers in a cunning and through deceptive ways that those who support politically the left and those who support politically the right as Toronto Staff reporters Ben Cohen and Joshua Chong label this conflict appropriately as "A World of Emotions" and also that the word of God backs this label up as well according to and in Proverbs 29: 27. This Genocidal Peace would also be spread out throughout the media worldwide and that those who have or will reject Christ being infidels of the Authorized King James Version Bible who are --- and will be calling those who are true Christians of the Authorized King James Version Bible, religious fanatics who will become martyrs for Christ according to Revelation 6: 9, 10, 11 and Revelation 20: 4 and Jeremiah 51: 49. Who are by then refusing this global I.D. registration known as a one world digital currency that is mentioned in the Bible as the Mark of the Beast according to Revelation 13: 14, 15, 16, 17, 18 and Revelation 14: 9, 10, 11.

CHAPTER 6
Desperate Dictators

What is the definition of a dictator? One who rules absolutely and often oppressively. An example of a desperate dictator is Saddam Hussein who may have had weapons of mass destruction and the means to deliver them? Senator Edward Kennedy, echoing the standard views of political scientists, has questioned the wisdom of pursuing regime change in Iraq by Military means. If a war to remove him is going well the argument goes that Saddam will see that he, personally is doomed, and will decide that he might as well inflict as much pain as he can on his enemies before he dies. The logic of pure reason says that you cannot deter a leader who has nothing to lose.

There are several things wrong with this argument. The first is history. This is not the first time a war has been waged to effect regime change against a leader who had weapons of mass destruction. Adolf Hitler's Third Reich had stock piles of nerve gas and a weakened but still effective military chain of command to execute his orders. But when the Red Army was entering Berlin, there were no clouds of Sarin or Tabun unleashed against the Soviet soldiers who would, without doubt, deal out the roughest kind of justice to Germany and Hitler himself. Not only that, but earlier in the war, Hitler's orders to destroy Paris as the Germans withdrew were not obeyed. As German defeat became more certain, even the killings of Jews and others in death camps were halted, at least for some periods of time.

Tyrants do not commit mass murder with their own hands. They have subjects who carry out their commands. Tyrants are obeyed because they are feared, and go to great lengths to ensure that their subjects fear them more than they fear the external enemies of the regime. But when they begin to lose a total war, the balance of fear among those they have been oppressing begins to shift. People begin looking around them to see if it is safe to turn their coats, and defect or cause mutiny. If one prominent subordinate successfully disobeys orders, others learn the lesson and act accordingly, creating a cascade of increasing numbers of defections. This is why dictatorships that seem so solid can so rapidly fall apart when the first cracks in the regime become publicly visible. In a regime guilty of crimes against humanity, subordinates will not want to be taken prisoner while in the act of committing mass murder, defending a tyrant who is on the verge of total defeat.

Logically, this suggests that tyrants might unleash their stockpiles of weapons of mass destruction before it is obvious to their subordinates, that they will be overthrown. If Saddam Hussein saw the inevitable coming early enough, he could order his remaining SCUDs loaded with biological weapons and have them launched against Israel, by generals who still feared him more than the American armies that might falter by the burden of war before they got to Baghdad.

This overlooks another major characteristic of tyrants. they tend to have hefty amounts of self- confidence. They have after, all gained and held absolute power against all comers. They have survived attempts to kill or defeat them. They have difficulty believing they can lose or are also being over confident according to Proverbs 14: 16. Hitler when hearing of the death of Franklin Roosevelt in April 1945 cheered himself up the thought that, like Frederick the Great, he would still pull through because a key adversary had died. In addition, tyrants are not surrounded by people who bring them down to earth according to Proverbs 15: 22, 31, 32, 33.

All the evidence we have from the Hitler, Stalin and Mao regimes shows that their subordinates did not present, but rather concealed, information that revealed the ongoing failure policies ordered by the tyrant. The subordinates of the tyrant know, long before the tyrant is forced to believe, that the game is up. The idea that men like Saddam Hussein will believe that they are doomed, and order apocalyptic action before the very last moment, is to ignore everything we know about the most basic part of their personalities.

If what has been written here about tyrants is correct, there are some clear policy implications for the United States as it may plan its war against another tyrant like Saddam Hussein or Vladimir Putin. First, we should say, publicly and often, that those who forbear will be treated mercifully. We should state publicly that we know that Saddam Hussein has given commanders operational control of chemical and biological weapons, so that if the weapons are used, it is because of the actions of local commanders who will be held accountable. It comes as no surprise that those who carry out these atrocities for tyrants or desperate dictators will be held accountable. For if it was not for these people who follow the orders of a tyrant or desperate dictator --- dictators or tyrants would have no power to oppress the civilians in their regimes. But the problems to attack or try to get rid of a tyrant or desperate dictator with weapons of mass destruction are real but not insuperable or not having that capability that we are able to overcome it. Here there is only one thing that stands between a dictator and those who do not like oppression and that is more than one country or regime --- because as history has shown that empires of the past have risen and fallen because tyrants or desperate dictators are powerful oppressors, and causing oppression always and creates enemies one way or another because how can Satan cast out Satan? And if a kingdom is divided against itself, that kingdom cannot stand as mentioned here in the Authorized King James Version Bible according to Mark 3: 23, 24, 25, 26.

But in our world today we have a coming One World Government with an Antichrist dictator known also as the Beast that is a different scenario who cannot be overthrown but by God's prophetic plans and by divine intervention. Since the Antichrist or Beast would be the only leader of a One World Government and would have no opposing leader who is not considered in the political realm of being in dictatorship mode. It's true the Antichrist would be able to rule the planet --- but that would be from the aid of other dictators or known in the Bible as the "10 kings" of a confederacy of 10 nations that are all under a dictatorship or a tyrant known as the Antichrist or Beast according to Revelation 17: 12, 13.

And these 10 kings would help merge this world leader or tyrant or dictator or Antichrist or Beast into a position of world leadership of authority and by tyrannical means of dominating the rest of the world through and by these other 10 kings or dictators. And so, to overthrow this Antichrist it would have to take having a conflict with another dictator where here a dictator is known to not have a conscience to the point that two world dictators in a conflict would be a complete menace to civilization that would lead to Armageddon. Here desperate dictators are known to deceive the populace or the masses in order to succeed with committing genocide for the purpose of bringing an attempted shot at permanent peace to communities in order for them to secure their empire of oppression for the purpose of control and achieving a lavish lifestyle for themselves and for their nearest associates or colleagues in the adjacent political dictatorship realm.

There has also been individualized desperate dictators in Hama's military who have committed horrible atrocities of Rape and murder. This genocide and rape and these isolated murders and rape in Israel has been mentioned in the Authorized King James Version Bible as the pretty women who have rejected Christ and have been raped or ravished by Hamas military members where these women and their punishment because of their sins and that their inheritance is turned to strangers and their houses invaded by aliens or by the Hamas military is also mentioned in all of Chapter 5 in the book of Lamentations. Here because of these atrocities against these women that were raped and killed, they were also pardoned for their sins after these judgments that fell upon them by the wicked or indirectly by God; since the judgments of rape and death are indirectly carried out by God through the wicked. And after these judgments their sins or iniquity are also pardoned by God according to Isaiah 40: 1, 2.

A Former White House Counsel John Dean said on CNN on January 7th / 2024 that Donald Trump does not have a conscience unlike Richard Nixon who was perhaps not one to cross certain boundaries like Donald Trump has. Trump has also said that the civil war could have been negotiated. Trump has also said that the FBI organized the January 6th / 2021 riot at the U.S. Capitol. The U.S. Capitol is the most recognized symbol of democratic government in the world. The United States Capitol has housed Congress since 1800. The Capitol is where Congress meets to write the laws of the nation in the U.S. And is also where presidents are inaugurated and deliver their annual State of the Union messages.

There are also judges or magistrates on the bench who may be also considered desperate dictators who have in the past had condemned the innocent according to Psalms 94: 20, 21. I had a decent judge by the name of Hughe Locke. Whom I failed to mention in my book "Immunity From Prosecution." I remember at my Ontario Review Board hearing in 2005 that I mentioned to him that I have read some of the Toronto Star news clippings that mentioned Judge Hughe Locke and how the clippings described comments he made just before he would find the defendant guilty or sentence him to hard time for the serious felony he had committed. Then I remember that Hughe Locke said to me quote: "Well I got something also for you to sign Mr. Bazzanella" --- Then I responded humbly by saying quote: "Its O.K. your honour but I would also like to even get your signature." Judge Hughe Locke knew that there is no respect of persons according to Colossians 3: 25. And he knew also that I had spent from 1983 October to 2005 incarcerated in and out of Psychiatric institutions and where I had no prior criminal or psychiatric record before this crime of Attempted Murder on a police officer where I rammed a police cruiser where no one was killed and where no one was hurt in this crime and where at the time in 2005 I was a normal Forensic Psychiatric patient who had not done much or had not written and published any books back then and therefore was granted an Absolute Discharge at my 2005 hearing as he was presiding at my 2005 Ontario Review Board hearing being a retired Judge from the Bench.

Judge Hughe Locke had made the right decision even though I had re-offended after this by committing a break and enter by breaking the glass door of an Equipment Rental All facility stealing a chainsaw. I was messed up on the psychiatric drugs at that particular time and was forced to take these psychiatric drugs that were tormenting me, that led to me re-offending in the community. And so I blame the psychiatrists for provoking me by forcing these drugs on me with security guards present to administer injections of this psychiatric drug called "Haldol" which has a side effect of causing vision impairment or blindness; and of the psychiatric drug called "Invega" that has a side effect of causing blood clots that has led to a stroke and could lead to another stroke in the future. So when I constantly and explicitly complained about these drugs causing harm I was still forced to take these drugs where now after 40 years of this unjust psychiatric treatment and abuse by these harmful psychiatric drugs that I am on now, that I now have been left blind in my left eye and I have now stage 3 kidney damage in February 2024 and where I also experienced a stroke on May 8th / 2022.

On CP-24 news in Toronto on February 23rd / 2024 it was mentioned that Donald Trump wants to bring back Christianity --- this is propaganda in order to successfully achieve a formation of a one world government under one world leader, that will be known in the Bible as the Antichrist or Beast and not known or recognized by the populace or the masses worldwide in numbers who are the god of this world with a small "g" according to 2nd Corinthians 4: 4.

Here this world leader who may be Donald Trump or his successor who both may or will possibly be of a Religious Apostate Babylonian Christianity mindset that is completely secular in nature.

And here this one world Government will have the ambassadors of the 10 king dictators of the Antichrist or Beast according to Revelation 17: 12, 13 who are each ruling these 10 separate global regions on planet earth headed up by the Antichrist or Beast ---- that will have these ambassadors possibly ask John Bazzanella to enquire as to what has happened in the land regarding the wars and atrocities that has taken place in Ukraine and Israel according to 2nd Chronicles 32: 31 after revealing the prophecies of the Authorized King James Version Bible related to world events. Which has sparked these atrocities and wars in Ukraine and Israel resulting in the rise of antisemitism where I may be accused of causing these atrocities and wars in Ukraine and Israel because of revealing these Biblical prophecies related to world events and because of the Biblical Rhetoric expressed in my books that are published and being sold online and letters and emails sent to the media. And these books I have written and had published and the emails and letters also sent to Journalists and Reporters and Celebrities and Politicians on a worldwide scale causing strife and contention to the whole earth according to Jeremiah 15: 10.

Here antisemitism has existed before I was born, since Israel became a nation in 1948 and long before this, did antisemitism exist. Here I may be also sentenced to a furnace by the Babylonian Apostate Religious Politicians because of this written Biblical Rhetoric of the Authorized King James Version Bible that may have caused the wars and atrocities in Ukraine and Israel showing to the world that I am not a servant of God but a false servant of God in order to pave a peaceful way for their One World Government claiming to and promising to restore peace and prosperity to the world saying that, people like me who don't believe in peace should be eliminated from societal norm of living in harmony with others. Here I may be sentenced by desperate dictators to a furnace, for perdition of civilization according to John 17: 12. When I am sentenced to that furnace? Is that also here again no prophecy of scripture is of any private interpretation according to 2nd Peter 1: 20.

What will happen in that furnace? Will I be delivered and be redeemed according to Jeremiah 15: 21? Here in this Scripture the term "redeem" may refer to redemption or rescue from a dangerous predicament or situation. But I may burn before I am redeemed or receive redemption into immortality according to 1st Timothy 6: 14, 15, 16. Since at the time I am sentenced I may be a mere mortal where the rapture and resurrection into immortality may have not taken place yet. Until I have entered into that furnace during this furnace sentence where a long or brief moment of possible excruciating chastisement of burning would take place while I am in that furnace, just before I am resurrected or redeemed into immortality. Where here the affliction of incendiary chastisement where the fire that is kindled in God's Anger which shall burn upon me will no longer have any effect on me where I would not feel any mild or serious or excruciating burning sensation after this resurrection or redemption takes place in that furnace according to Jeremiah 15: 14, 21.

Here also the reason Donald Trump may be that coming Antichrist is because he is flattering those voters who have been indicted or convicted of a crime. Here Donald Trump; as he claims has received bias or prejudice indictments which he has compared these indictments that he claims are bias or prejudice to those who are Black Americans who also experienced these bias or prejudice indictments in the U.S. legal system. Here former president Donald Trump claimed that his four criminal indictments have boosted his support among Black Americans because they see him as a victim of discrimination, comparing his legal jeopardy to the historic legacy of anti-Black prejudice in the U.S. legal system. Here he is flattering a large portion of Black American Voters, and voters in general, because of these claims of discrimination. And he may very well be this coming Little Horn or coming Antichrist or Beast who is obtaining this coming kingdom of a brief and temporary and short lived one world government by flatteries which shall come to an end eventually according to Daniel 11: 21, 44, 45.

Also as a desperate dictator like Vladimir Putin he will continue to go on a killing rampage in this invasion of Ukraine because he has mocked

Christianity of the Authorized King James Version Bible because my God or the God of the Christians of the Authorized King James Version Bible who has allowed my physical condition to get a stroke and a get a blind left eye and get stage 3 kidney damage where these psychiatric drugs and their side effects caused this physical damage to my body and my health because of being forced to take these Psychiatric drugs with security guards present, in case I refuse the injection of these psychiatric drugs.

And that I have also become incarcerated for an excessive period of time of 40 years in and out of psychiatric institutions. Where here Vladimir Putin is deceived into thinking that there is no God. And where here God sends him a deception and who Putin believes not in the truth but has pleasure in unrighteousness, so God sends Vladimir Putin a strong delusion that he should believe this lie that I am not getting healed by God and I have not received any blessings from God but constant and ongoing suffering and where Vladimir Putin also believes this lie that God doesn't exist where he is in unbelief of this existence of this God of the Authorized King James Version Bible according to 2nd Thessalonians 2: 10, 11, 12.

CHAPTER 7
Haughty Psychology

Some people like to be on top and berate others who may have been men of low estate who have succeeded later in life humiliating those of a lower profile and reputation that have all along been of the examples of these desperate dictators that have succeeded in taking control of others, that I have described here in chapter 6. They certainly because of their haughty behaviour and being these conceited desperate dictators don't want to condescend to men like myself of low estate according to Romans 12: 16.

These people can have or be of a haughty spirit and tend to fall eventually. One example is that some tend to in some cases to be haughty in spirit. That causes man that has the iniquity of pride to sin where the result of this haughty spirit of sin results in either destruction or the chastisement by God or also in some cases cruel chastisement. Like in my case where I experienced this cruel chastisement causing me to become blind in my left eye by being forced to take a harmful psychiatric drug known and called "Haldol" and also known to have side effects like giving me impaired vision problems or that caused blindness according to Matthew 6: 22 and Proverbs 18: 12 and Jeremiah 30: 13, 14, 15 and Hebrews 12: 6, 7, 8, 9, 10, 11. Also my previous psychiatrist named Dr. Georgia Walton had only damaged my optic nerve with this psychiatric medication called "Haldol" that was forced on me by injection with security guards present if I were to refuse the injection.

Also, the reason this damage took place was because of my haughty and verbal negative attitude towards blaming psychiatrists and psychiatric nurses for the treatment which I had received which was abusive in nature. Here a haughty spirit and loose lips leads to destruction according Proverbs 18: 6, 7, 12. Here the term "strokes" refers according to the James Strong's Exhaustive Concordance of the Bible, Old Testament # 4112 from # 1986 as a "blow" or "stripe" or "stroke" or "to strike down" or "to hammer, stamp, conquer, disband," or "beat down" or break down, overcome, smite (with a hammer). Here this type of "stroke" or calling for mocking and criticism from your adversaries from having loose lips has also led to strife and contention between me and my caregivers in these psychiatric institutions especially here in CAMH psychiatric institution in Toronto according to Jeremiah 15: 10.

Also, these "strokes" or "stroke" calling for this verbal conflict between me and my caregivers has caused this abusive damage that was done by my caregivers and the psychiatrists who were treating me with this psychiatric drug called "Haldol" which affected the optic nerve and had only distorted my vision. But I was not blinded by this optic nerve damage. Also, this psychiatrist Dr. Georgia Walton of CAMH psychiatric institution in Toronto also sent me to an optometrist on May 2nd / 2022 who blinded me further in my left eye by deliberately shining the diagnostic examination light for a prolong period of time on my left eye's retina causing permanent blindness. And this permanent blindness was because my retina in my left eye was damaged and therefore there was no one to plead my cause of this abuse by my psychiatrist Dr. Georgia Walton or by the optometrist who was either Dr. Dang or Dr. Chu that she sent me to, who abused me as well. And there was no one here to plead my cause for me to fight them in a court of law for this serious abuse; or to fight them in a court of law for a lawsuit for this serious abuse of this deliberate damage that had been done to my retina in my left eye. Because this serious abuse is difficult to prove since a psychiatric patient is not credible in a lawsuit against a qualified psychiatrist or a qualified optometrist and there is no healing medicine to heal my retina since it is not possible to correct a retina once it is damaged or become detached from the back of the interior of the eyeball according to Jeremiah 30: 13.

Here Dr. Georgia Walton may have been troubled by the fact that I would sue her for the optic nerve damage and may have colluded with either Dr. Dang or Dr. Chu who did my eye examine who are the optometrists at King Eye West Care clinic at 1008 King St. West in Toronto. Where here either Dr. Dang or Dr. Chu who deliberately blinded my left eye's retina with the examination light in order to find my previous psychiatrist Dr. Georgia Walton not guilty in this lawsuit that I may have planned against her.

Since here also is that the optometrist may have planned in court to testify against me claiming I must have looked at the sun too long. When in fact he was the one who blinded me deliberately with the examination diagnostic light. And so, this optometrist was unscrupulously claiming that

I must have looked at the sun too long that caused me to go completely blind. And that this was the cause for me complaining about my eye sight. And not my complaint of my optic nerve that was giving me this distorted vision. But instead that I was blinded by the sun that damaged my left eye's retina and that the psychiatric drug "Haldol" that damaged my optic nerve was not the case.

Claiming as well that I may have been delusional believing and complaining that my vision was distorted by the damage done to the optic nerve by this psychiatric drug called "Haldol" and testifying in court that I must of looked at the sun too long and that this may have been the reason for the damage to my left eye claiming my left eye's retina may have been damaged by looking at the sun too long and therefore acquitting my psychiatrist Dr. Georgia Walton from a lawsuit that I may have wanted to file against her in a court of law for my claim of the damage done to the optic nerve of my left eye by this psychiatric drug called "Haldol."

What was the reasons for all of these problems I have mentioned here that I have experienced regarding this psychiatric treatment done to me by Dr. Walton? Was it envy and jealousy by Dr. Georgia Walton of CAMH psychiatric institution? Was this envy and jealousy committed against me by Dr. Walton and Dr. Dang and Dr. Chu because of her and Dr. Dang and Dr. Chu having a haughty spirit and attitude towards me because I had written my first book on the Bible related to world events called "Pyromancy." Which was published and being sold online on Amazon and other bookstores worldwide near the end of December / 2021 and in the beginning of January / 2022?

Here haughtiness is not to be confused with pride of self-love, these two passions or attitudes are very different in their nature and in their effects. Self-Love or pride using discretion is a natural sentiment which prompts every animal to watch over its own conservation ... Pride is only a relative, artificial sentiment born in society, a sentiment which prompts each individual to attach more importance to himself than to anyone else........ Rousseau (1754 / 1984, p. 167).

Pride is an important emotion that plays a critical role in many domains of psychological functioning. In particular, feelings of pride can reinforce prosocial behaviours such as altruism or unselfish regard or for the devotion to the welfare of others and adaptive behaviours such as achievement (Hart & Matsuba, in press; Weiner, 1985). The loss of pride is part of what provokes aggression and other antisocial behaviours in response to ego threats (Bushman & Baumeister, 1998). The regulation of pride is intrinsically linked to self-esteem regulation and maintenance; many acts of self-enhancement are likely attempting to increase one's feelings of pride. In fact, pride is the primary emotion (along with shame) that gives self-esteem its affective kick (J.D. Brown & Marshall, 2001), and self-esteem in turn influences a wide range of intrapsychic or occurring within the psyche or mind or personality and interpersonal processes or that are relating to and interacting in relationships with others.

Despite its centrality to social behaviour, pride has received little attention in the social-personality literature, even relative to other self-conscious emotions such as shame and guilt. Here Pride is ignored for the treatment and rehabilitation or psychiatric patients who have anti-social behaviours where here excessive pride poses a problem or causes anger or aggression or conflict between people in general. The reason Pride is not an issue as a psychiatric problem may be because psychiatry may have people who are extremely proud of their profession as a psychiatrist or psychiatric worker which gives these people a sense of pride and having that arrogance of the fact that they feel they are not vulnerable like those who suffer from a psychiatric disorder and viewing them as a lower form of man. Here psychiatry does not address excessive pride because most of those in psychiatry may be guilty of having excessive pride and therefore ignore addressing this issue of excessive pride as a psychological problem.

Here a lack of pride causes people who have excessive pride to mock or criticize others who have a lack of pride and are considered outcasts in society because they may not feel worthy enough to socialize with those who through more achievements by pride, have gained a respect that has caused them to have a decent sense of pride. Here the lack of pride because of failure may provoke those who have this lack of pride to commit crimes of retribution like mass murders. Like these mass shootings that have taken place within the last 30 years or so. Here a good example is the Russian Leader Vladimir Putin who caused all these atrocities in Ukraine. Which may have provoked him to cause these atrocities because most of the world has criticized him as a failure and dishonorable leader and some even called him a despicable murderer.

Vladimir Putin's haughty attitude has brought him to a point that he is threatening nuclear war as mentioned on in the media on March 1st / 2024. Here Putin warns that the West is risking nuclear war. And that Putin has vowed to fulfill Moscow's goals in Ukraine and sternly warned the West against deeper involvement in the fighting, saying that such a move is fraught with the risk of a global nuclear conflict. Putin's blunt warning came in a state of the nation address ahead of the Russian election where he is all but certain to win, underlining his readiness to raise the stakes in the tug of war with the West to protect the Russian gains in Ukraine. Here Putin has a haughty attitude where his confidence of gaining ground in this Ukraine war has given him this mentality of either risk losing this war and be found to be guilty at the International Criminal Court for crimes against humanity or win the war, or die trying, and taking the whole planet with him in this nuclear devastation he is about to unleash on the world in order to avoid total defeat in this war in Ukraine.

Will he be elected for more terms as the president of Russia? As of this writing on March 2nd / 2024 it is not known. But there are Many Russians in his country that don't agree with this war and his invasion of Ukraine and the severe and horrific suffering he has inflicted on Ukraine and may have also influenced that devastating war in Israel and the absolute horrific suffering that these atrocities have caused in both these two wars. If he is elected it will be based not on the votes of the Russian citizens, but of a corrupt electoral system. Here Russians officials first employed multiple-day voting in the 2020 referendum. Putin orchestrated to push a constitutional reform that would allow him to run for two more terms. However, this will be the first time that multi-day voting will be used in a presidential vote. It will also be the first presidential election in which voters can cast ballots online, with e-voting rolled out across 29 regions.

Independent election observers widely criticized stretching the vote for several days and allowing online voting, saying they were tactics to further hinder the transparency of the balloting process. Opposition groups in 2021 said digital votes in the country's parliamentary elections showed signs of manipulation.

Being Haughty like Vladimir Putin has been; and has also attracted those who despise his attitude. Furthermore, a Haughty attitude is totally tainted with absolute arrogance and lawlessness to the point that he believes he is invincible. And if he believes this, where here Putin succeeds in forming this Babylonian Religious Apostate worldwide economic and political empire, then if humanity cannot eradicate him and eradicate those who supported him and who fought for him in this Ukraine war; then God will come along with his servant to eradicate Putin and those who are all his supporters and are the adversaries of a just humanity and the adversaries of the God of the Authorized King James Version Bible according to Hebrews 10: 27 and Daniel 7: 11.

Here our God is terrible majesty even the weather like tornados and hurricanes submit to him and God does not respect any man who is wise of heart like Vladimir Putin according to Job 37: 21 22, 23, 24. Here Vladimir Putin is believing foolishly that he can conquer the world by destroying others and having them killed in order to bring peace which is known as Genocidal Peace as I have titled this book. For by peace he shall destroy many and shall be broken without the hand of war and conflict in a furnace that he prepares for those who do not support him in this One World Government that he will rule with other dictators or be one of the 10 kings giving that tyrannical power to the Antichrist or Beast who may be Donald Trump according to Daniel 8: 23, 24, 25 and Revelation 17: 12, 13.

And also building a furnace for others he plans on burning alive in this despotic ruling kingdom of the Antichrist or Beast and he shall hang himself in all of this after he hanged or had killed a lot of Jews and like Haman would have had done to a Jew like Mordecai. If he is not afraid now of God's majesty, Putin will be afraid later as this judgment of a furnace that he plans on building along with those dictators who support him in order to sentence and burn alive others. And so those dictators who have supported Putin will turn on him and eventually sentence him to death by hanging him by death in this furnace according to Esther 7: 6, 7, 8, 9, 10.

How will this situation come about? It will take place only if a servant of God is delivered by God from this furnace that was built by Putin and his supporters in order to sentence this servant of God and others who have offended humanity with mass killings that resulted in the end in horrible iniquity that will be sentenced to this furnace that is perhaps developed and built by Putin and who are against his One World Government of the Antichrist or Beast and who are, and will be sentenced to a furnace according to Matthew 13: 41, 42. Where here also Donald Trump may be ruling this despotic One World Government of this Antichrist or Beast where here this servant of God may be delivered out of that furnace by God according to Jeremiah 15: 14, 21 and Matthew 13: 43.

CHAPTER 8
Haughtiness Spawns Humiliation

To be haughty is to also to go about by the establishment of being dishonored where being haughty displays an arrogant and proud attitude which leads to spawning a reputation that leads to becoming a victim of humiliation according to Proverbs 18: 12. Here a story in "The New York Times" called "Predators Leer at Girls' Instagram Photos". Where mother's boast about the physical appearance of their daughters. Here ominous messages began arriving in Elissa's inbox early last year. "You sell pics of your underage daughter to pedophiles," read one. "you're such a naughty sick mom, you're just as sick as us pedophiles," read another. "I will make life hell for you and your daughter."

Elissa has been running her daughter's Instagram account since 2020, when the girl was 11 years old. Photos show a bright bubbly girl modeling evening dresses, high end workout gear and dance leotards. She has more than 100,000 followers, some so enthusiastic about her posts that they pay $ 9.99 dollars a month for more photos.

Here Elissa has fielded all kinds of criticism and knows that some people think she is exploiting her daughter. She has even gotten used to receiving creepy messages, but these, from "Instamodelfan" were extreme. I think they're all pedophiles, she said of the many online followers boasting here about her daughter's appearance.

Here in Proverbs 18: 12 it says Quote: "Before destruction the heart of man is haughty, and before honour is humility."

This destruction could indicate that her daughter could be in harm's way or even be killed. Here what starts out as boastful pride of your daughter's physical appearance and trying to achieve easy financial success and popularity for their daughter is what often starts as parents offer to jump start a child's modeling career, or win favors from clothing brands, can quickly descend into a dark underworld dominated by adult men, many of whom openly admit other platforms to being sexually attracted to children, an investigation by The New York Times has found.

Thousands of accounts examined by the New York Times offer disturbing insights into how social media is reshaping childhood, especially for girls, with direct parental involvement. Some parents are the driving force behind the sale of photos, exclusive chat sessions and even the girls' worn outfits to followers. The most devoted customers spend thousands of dollars nurturing the underage relationships. The large audience boosted by men can benefit the families; the New York Times found. The bigger followings look impressive to brands and bolster chances of getting products and other financial incentives, and the accounts themselves are rewarded by Instagram's algorithm with greater visibility, which in turn attracts more followers. One calculation performed by an audience demographics firm found 32 million connections to make followers among the 5,000 accounts examined by the New York Times.

Here interacting with men opens the doors to abuse. Some flatter, bully and blackmail girls and their parents to get racier images. The New York times monitored separate exchanges on Telegram, the messaging app, were men openly fantasize about sexually abusing the children they follow on Instagram and extol or praise these child accounts or the platforms for making images available. Nearly 1 in 3 preteens list influencing as a career goal, and 11 percent of those born in Generation Z, between 1997 and 2012, describe themselves as influencers. The so-called creator economy surpasses 250 billion dollars worldwide, according to Goldman Sachs, with U.S. brands spending over 5 billion dollars a year on these Generation Z influencers.

But health and technology experts have recently cautioned that social media presents a "profound risk of harm" for these girls. The pursuit of fame, particularly through Instagram, has supercharged the often-toxic phenomenon, the New York Times found. Encouraging parents to commodify their children's images. Some child influencers earn over 100,000 dollars a year according to interviews.

A parent said "I really don't want my child exploited on the internet," said Kaelyn, a mother in Melbourne, Australia, who like many parents interviewed by the New York Times agreed to be identified only by a middle name. But she has been doing this so long now. Her monetary numbers are so big? What do we do? Just stop and walk away? Large amounts of money are always attractive to those who want to become popular since large sums of money is tied to fame and glory. If this were not the case then money is not attractive to those who just want to get by and avoid a haughty and proud tactic to achieve quick financial success and boast about this success.

After all these people who exploit their children, is that, they feel that their underaged children will grow into maturity in a few short years and get them off the hook of being these sick parents who are worse than pedophiles and then when their children do get to the age of consent and maturity that all will be forgotten and they can then move on with their lives having large sums of money in the bank and get their young daughters a good life and get them married and have children and then they can become grandparents.

But being haughty and proud of your daughter's appearance is risky business when money is involved because being in a position where you exploit your daughter for money in the beginning and not being familiar with the world of fame and celebrities is where established celebrities with millions of dollars has many friends in the high places like having judges in the criminal courts as close friends. Where if you are a new comer after being poor you don't have a chance to plead your case if an issue like rape arises against your daughter where you achieved to get her a modelling career, making large sums of money. Because powerful people with millions of dollars would have many friends.

Where you being a parent who tried to achieve success after being poor that these powerful people have many friends in the high places and would not be prosecuted for whatever crime is committed against you, or your child or young teen daughter, who is an upcoming model. Also those who have been recently poor are separated from their friends that they had when they were poor and would not be able to get help from them, since these who are the filthy rich after they have had many friends in the high places after being rich and well established for many years will be at an advantage legally and financially against these foolish and vulnerable parents who have exploited their children for financial gain according to

Proverbs 19: 1, 2, 3 ,4 and Proverbs 14: 20.

Meta, the Instagram's parent's company, found that 500,000 child Instagram accounts had "inappropriate" interactions every day, according to an internal study in 2020 quoted in legal proceedings. In a statement to the New York Times Andy Stone, a Meta Spokesperson, said that parents were responsible for the accounts and could delete them anytime. Anyone on Instagram can control who is able to tag, mention or message them, as well, as who can comment on their account " Andy Stone has added.

Like many parents, Elissa said she protected her daughter by handling the account exclusively herself. Ultimately, she concluded the Instagram community is dominated by "disgusting creeps" but she nonetheless keeps the account up and running. She also said that shutting it down would be giving in to bullies. Here it may not only be celebrities with lots of money but those who are in poverty or those who have an obsession with young girls where these parents could have their daughter's physical identity be revealed in a public domain and therefore risking the security of their child or very young daughter to these so called pedophiles or as Elissa has said of these "disgusting creeps."

In today's creator economy, companies often turn to social media influencers to attract new customers. In the dance and gymnastics worlds, teens and preteen jockey to become brand ambassadors, they don bikinis in Instagram posts, walk runways in youth fashion shows and offer paid subscriptions to videos showing their everyday going- on.

The most successful girls can demand 3,000 dollars from sponsors for a single post, but monetary gain can be elusive for others. Youth fashion shows charge the girls to participate and charge their parents to attend. In 2022 Instagram launched paid subscriptions which allows followers to pay a monthly fee for exclusive content and access. The rules do not allow subscriptions for anyone under 18, but the mom-run accounts sidestep that restriction. The times found dozens that charged from 99 cents to $ 19.99. At the highest price, parents offered "ask me anything" chat sessions and behind the scene photos.

Child safety experts warn the subscriptions could lead to unhealthy interactions. I have reservations about a child feeling like they have to satisfy either adults in their orbit or strangers who are asking something from them, said Sally Theran, a psychology professor at Wellesley College in Massachusetts.

For many mom-run accounts from men are a recurring scourge to be eradicated, or a fact of life to be ignored. For others, they are a source to be tapped. "The first thing I do when I wake up and the last thing I do when I go to bed is block accounts" said Lynn, the mother of a 6-year-old girl in Florida who has about 3,000 followers from the dance world. The vast world of child influencer followers on Instagram includes men who have been convicted of sex crimes, and those who engage in forums off platforms where child sexual abuse imagery, including of girls on Instagram, is shared.

In monitoring multiple Telegram chat rooms; the New York Times found men who treat children's Instagram pages and subscription services as menus to satisfy their fantasies. They trade information about parents considered receptive to selling "private sets" of images. A group with over 4,000 members was highly organized, tracking nearly 700 children. The New York Times asked the Canadian Center for Child Protection, a group that monitors online child exploitation, to review links and other potentially illegal material posted by the Telegram groups and elsewhere. The center identified child sexual abuse imagery involving multiple underage Instagram models from around the world, as well as sexualized videos of others, including a preteen girl wearing a thong and a young teenager raising her dress to show her bikini bottom.

Men in these groups frequently praise the advent of Instagram as a golden age for child exploitation. "I'm so glad for these new moms pimping their daughters out," one of them wrote.

A small group of men cultivate business and patronage relationships with mothers. One man tries to persuade a mother to sell her daughter's leotards because many men including himself were "collector " according to a recording of the conversation. "In retrospect I feel like such a stupid mom, but I'm not stupid" said a mother of a young gymnast who dealt with similar men before she realized they were predators. "I didn't understand what grooming was."

Meta failed to act on multiple reports made by parents and even restricted those who tried to police their own followers, according to interviews and materials provided by the parents. If they block too many followers' accounts in a day Meta curtails their ability to block or follow others, they said. "I remember being told like I have reached my limit," said a mother of two dancers in Arizona who declined to be named. "Like what? I Reached my limit of pedophiles for today."

Mr. Stone the Meta spokesperson, said, "there are lots of reasons an account might face limitations or restrictions and therefore it was difficult to know why parents encounter these problems." One parent reported a photo of erect male genitalia sent in a direct message. Another reported an account that reposted children's photos with explicit or clearly revealed and expressed captions. A third reported a user who propositioned her child for sex offering 65,000 dollars for "an hour" with the girl. In response to those three reports Meta said either that the communications did not violate "Community guidelines" or that its staff did not have time to review them.

Here you want to make easy money using your daughter as an object for revenue? And these moms or parents having a sense of haughty behavior boasting about their daughter's pretty appearance online? Obviously, Meta has a point and is far too busy to deal with these types of accounts. Why not use these accounts to promote your daughter's connections to the community with friendships instead of exploiting them as models and boasting about how pretty your daughter is in a dress to the online world. We have known for years now about online scams and sexual predators having their presence online and how they prey on children or preteens who may also have an online presence. So, these moms have no cloak for their guilt of posting their children online for monetary gain. Here after these parents are committing their children to this online activity, they have the nerve and the audacity to expect protection from Meta authorities for these parents who are exploiting their children who are making these monetary gains for their parents. If you are going to be haughty then expect this destruction of exploitation where Meta authorities are unable to bear their wounded spirit because of these many online pedophiles and predators in over whelming numbers according to Proverbs 18: 12, 13, 14 Here former Meta trust and safety employees described an organization overwhelmed despite knowing about the problems for years. Here "You hear," "I reported this account, it was harassing my daughter, why is he back?" said a former investigator for the company who requested anonymity. There are not enough people, and resources and systems to tackle all of it.

We have a story here from the New York Times of the headquarters for gangs in prison? In Mexico City in January Ecuador's military was sent in to seize control of the country's prison after two major gang leaders escaped and criminal groups set off a nationwide revolt that paralyzed the country. In Brazil two inmates with connections to a major gang became the first to escape from one of the nation's five maximum-security federal prisons, officials said. In Colombia, officials declared an emergency in its prisons after two guards were killed and several more targeted in what the government said was retaliation for its crackdown on major criminal groups. Inside prisons across Latin America, criminal groups exercise unchallenged authority over prisoners, extracting money from them or basic necessities like food. The prisons also act as a safe haven for incarcerated criminal leaders to remotely run their criminal enterprises on the outside, ordering killings, and orchestrating the smuggling of drugs to the United States and Europe, and directing kidnappings and extortion of local businesses.

When officials attempt to curtail the power criminal groups exercise from behind bars, their leaders often deploy members on the outside to fight back. "The principal center of gravity, the nexus of control or organized crime, lies within the prison compounds," said Mario Pazmino, a retired colonel and former director of intelligence for Ecuador's Army. That's where let's say the management positions are, the command positions, he added. "It is where they give the orders and dispensations for gangs to terrorize the country."

Latin America's prison population has exploded over the last two decades, driven by stricter crime measures like pretrial detentions, but governments across the region have not spent enough to handle the surge instead have often relinquished control to inmates, experts on the penal system say.

Those sent to prison are often left with a choice: join a gang or face their wrath. This type of condition or atmosphere is no place for a forensic psychiatric patient. I would be killed in a place like this in these dangerous Latin prisons since I have never stabbed anyone or killed anyone. As a result, prisons have become crucial recruitment centers for Latin America's largest and most violent cartels and gangs, strengthening their grip on society instead of weakening it. Prison officials, who are underfunded, outnumbered, overwhelmed and frequently paid off, have largely given in to gang leaders in many prisons in exchange for a fragile peace. Criminal groups fully or partly control well over half of Mexico's 285 prisons, according to experts, while in Brazil the government often divides up penitentiaries based on gang affiliation in a bid to avoid unrest. In Ecuador, experts say most of the country's 36 prisons are under some degree of gang control. Latin America's prison population surged by 76 percent from 2010 to 2020, according to the Inter- American Development Bank, far exceeding the region's 10 percent population increase during the same period.

Many countries have imposed tougher law and order policies, including longer sentences and more convictions for low-level drug offenses pushing most of the region's penitentiaries beyond maximum capacity. At the same time, governments have prioritized investment in their security forces as a way to clamp down on crime and flex their muscles to the public, rather than spend on prisons which are less visible.

Brazil and Mexico, Latin America's largest countries with the region's biggest inmate populations, invest little on prisons: Brazil's government spends about 14 dollars per prisoner per day, while Mexico spends about 20 dollars per day. The United States spent about 117 dollars per prisoner per day in 2022. Prison guards in Latin America also earn meager salaries, making them susceptible to bribes from gangs to smuggle in contraband or help high-profile detainees escape. Officials in Brazil and Ecuador did not respond to requests for comment; officials in Mexico declined to comment. Underscoring the power of prison gangs' leaders live relatively comfortably behind bars, with new comfortable furniture much like having a living room in your own house; running supermarkets, cock fighting rings and nightclubs, and sometimes smuggling their families inside to stay with them.

In El Salvador, President Nayib Bukele declared a state of emergency in 2022 to tackle gang violence. About 75,000 people have been jailed, many without due process, according to human rights groups. Mr. Bukele's tactics have decimated the Central America country's street gangs, reversed years of horrific violence and helped propel him to a second term. But experts say thousands of innocent people have been incarcerated. What consequences does this have? said Carlos Ponce, an expert on El Salvador and assistant professor at the University of the Fraser Valley in Canada. "This will scar them and their families for life."

The frequent use of pretrial detentions across the region to combat crime has left many people languishing in jail for months and even years waiting to be tried, human rights groups say. The practice has fallen particularly hard on the poorest, who cannot afford lawyers and face a judicial system with cases backed up for years. In the first seven months of El Salvador's state of emergency, 84 percent of all those arrested were in pretrial detention and nearly half of Mexico's prison population is still awaiting trial. Elena Azola, a scholar in Mexico said, Prisons can be defined as exploitation centers for poor people.

Here these criminal gangs and cartels are in one sense better than the government who don't force street drugs on poor or rich ordinary citizens that go about their own business, like the government does --- forcing psychiatric drugs on people in psychiatric institutions. By forcing horrible psychiatric drugs that don't give people a feel-good high like street drugs do that these gangsters who deal out these drugs on the street that they have sold or given to people. Or sold or given to drug addicts who are those who abuse these street drugs themselves and die from an overdose. And then the drug dealers are held responsible for dealing these drugs and are charged and end up being convicted and doing many years on a prison term sentence. My question is why should they be held accountable and responsible? That's like asking a driver who is sober to be responsible for the actions of a drunk driver.

Here these psychiatric drugs instead make psychiatric patients vomit and destroying their kidneys and pancreas and liver and damaging your eye vision where I am now blind in my left eye and where I also suffered a stroke where these psychiatric drugs cause blood clots and where this damage is caused by constantly being given a dose of these psychiatric drugs every single day non-stop; by cowardly psychiatrists who have a haughty character that order an injection of these drugs by security guards in numbers for vulnerable patients, if these psychiatric patients who are not dangerous but defenseless refuses these psychiatric drugs. These psychiatrists are the real drug pushers and not the like the drug dealers on the street. Who these unscrupulous psychiatrists destroy lives according to being the real sorcerers and being the real drug pushers and liars according to Revelation 21: 8 and Revelation 22: 15 and Job 13: 4. The term "sorcerer" refers according to the Strong's Exhaustive Concordance of the Bible New Testament # 5331 from # 5332 as "medication" ("pharmacy") i.e. "magic" "sorcery" "witchcraft" (a drug, i.e. "spell giving potion") "a druggist" ("pharmacist") or poisoner, i.e. "a magician" "sorcerer."

I wonder how a haughty psychiatrist would treat a Latin gang and or a cartel member or anyone related to them eh? I bet there would be real humility after learning who these gang members are. Also, there are some forensic psychiatric patients in prisons and psychiatric institutions that have serious mental disorders that can make them extremely treacherous and dangerous but the treacherous ones would be diagnosed or labelled as a psycho-path with a disorder of being a potential deviant perpetrator and predator to their victims. Some are also sexual deviants who prey on their victims. Much like that serpent that is mentioned in the book of Genesis in the Authorized King James Version Bible that preyed on, and deceived Eve in the Garden of Eden according to Genesis 3: 1, 2, 3, 4, 5, and Genesis 3: 13.

A haughty spirit would deny the horrors that they fail to notice. Why would those who are haughty in spirit deny these horrors? Like psychiatrists who label sexual deviants as untreatable and don't force drugs on them like they would give drugs to innocent schizophrenic patients instead. Because they have the denial of a book called the Authorized King James Version Bible that reveals that excessive pride and the 7 deadly sins are a violation of God's commandments and statutes. Where we have to humbly submit to the God of this Bible and his judgments. The miraculous history of invention and productivity of our civilization is peppered with a multitude of dark stories of oppression, bloody wars, murder, and genocide which has now reached alarming levels in our civilization and in our near and far and or distant future and our near and far distant societies.

Also scams and fraud in our online world today is more than just a common occurrence but something we at some point in our lives do research on to learn how to avoid these online scams. The question is why were these horrors of atrocities, gruesome murders and murders in general and thefts by techniques of a devising theme like a scam even evolve to the point that we have to be on guard in a peaceful neighborhood. Or be aware online when we shop on a friendly appearing website, where if the price of the item is too low then it is probably too good to be true and is probably a scam waiting to happen to the most likely moral and just individual who is either letting their guard down or is a gullible person. Here we have lost globally in this world to 1.4 trillion dollars in scams.

How could we have lived with these atrocities and gruesome murders or murders in general or thefts or these recent online scams? A significant part of the reason for this points to the haughty spirit that man possesses and the rules that govern the spirit of man and his brain that has that difficult task to know what is right from wrong because we have been born in sin and have come short of the glory of God according to Romans 3: 23. Also, a significant part of the reason for this points to the rules that govern the operations of the human brain. Extreme political movements and deadly conflicts often escalate slowly. When threats start small and increase gradually, they end up eliciting a weaker reaction, amounting to less resistance and more acceptance because of a haughty dictator and those who possess this haughty behaviour who are being governed by this haughty dictator --- here these atrocities committed increase slowly and allows the larger and larger horrors to play out like conflicts like wars and the atrocities that follow these wars and criminal acts in the community that are often taken for granted and seen as ordinary occurrences and then the buck is passed to the next person and nothing gets done about these horrific issues that have the world in perilous times in these last days according to 2nd Timothy 3: 1, 2, 3, 4, 5.

One of us is a neuroscientist, the other is a law professor. From our different fields we have come to believe that it is not possible to understand the current period in which we live in now without appreciating why and how people do not notice of how much of what we live with that is now ignored or not noticed. The underlying reason is pivotal biological feature or our brain; here habituation or our tendency to respond less and less to things that change slowly tends to set in very slowly. An example is that you enter a cafe' filled with the smell of coffee at first the aroma is overwhelming but no more than 20 minutes and you cannot smell the coffee anymore and you have become accustomed to the strong aroma of coffee. This is our biological feature of our brain. Also being haughty makes this condition even worse because those who are haughty tend to not have humility to help those who are in serious distress and therefore they who are haughty also tend to become accustomed to their haughty behaviour and encouraged further by those of us who are humble who have the humility to help those who are victims of violence but also pass the buck to do anything about it and follow the lead of the masses; who some of them if not most of them are not humble but haughty. Here they are in numbers being the god with a small "g" of this world who have this haughty rejection of our Lord and savior Jesus Christ and refuse to give glory to the knowledge of God according to 2nd Corinthians 4: 4, 5, 6.

Human beings habituate to complex social circumstance such as war, oppression, misinformation and extremism. Habituation does not only result in a reduced tendency to notice immoral behavior or immoral deeds around us; it also increases the likelihood that we will engage in immoral behavior or deeds ourselves.

A famous study was conducted in the 1960's by psychologist Stanley Milgram, done to understand the rise of authoritarianism, as it happened in Germany before and during World War II. Milgram showed that regular citizens were willing to administer electric shock treatments --- even those that appeared painful --- to others when told to do so by an authority figure. Volunteers were asked to deliver small shocks, only very slowly, and by increment steps to ramp up the voltage.

By asking the volunteers to increase the voltage one step at a time, Milgram was inducing emotional habituation. They may have felt some guilt at first, but because the shocks increased by small increments, any feelings of guilt were likely less intense than they would otherwise have been. By the time the volunteers reached the high voltage, many appeared to have habituated to the idea of causing dreadful pain. This behavior makes these circumstances more severe when you have people who are haughty because excessive pride neglects others who may be in painful distress.

Milgram's study tells us about how people can get used to not only lying and cruelty, but also horrors --- including their own. You might now be thinking about alarming developments in the United States and Europe. If so, you are entirely right to do so. Here resistance, efforts often do emerge in response to injustice or horror; consider the French Resistance, the civil rights movement and # Me Too. These movements tend to be initiated by what might be called "dishabituation entrepreneurs." Those are people who have not habituated to the evils of their society; they both see the wrongdoing for what it is and call it out to cause dishabituation in others. Often dishabituation entrepreneurs are individuals who have experienced the horror or discrimination themselves, and refuse to get used to it. Malala Yousafzai, Mohandas Gandhi and Nelson Mandela are powerful examples.

Can dishabituation entrepreneurs be produced? We think so. A key is what John Stuart Mill once described as "experiments of living." Mill emphasized the importance of seeing one's beliefs, values, norms, and situations from a distance, to be able to evaluate them and perhaps learn that a change would be desirable. To do so we need to diversify our experiences. If people intentionally expose themselves to different cultures, different practices and different forms of government, then the injustices around them may no longer seem natural and inevitable. In words of the philosopher Abraham Joshua Heschel: "We must learn how to be surprised, not to adjust ourselves."

Here we must learn that to be surprised is the same as being and searching for something new and that this haughty behavior that man has is that it should be recognized not only among ourselves but to realize that others may possess the same negative attributes; so here the highway of the upright is to be of a humble spirit with the lowly and depart from evil than to divide the spoil with the proud that leads to destruction according to Proverbs 16: 17, 18, 19.

Also, the enlightenment philosopher Baruch Spinoza almost died for his ideals in 1672. Spinoza, a Sephardic Jew or a Jew who was from a region of Sepharad where Jews were once exiled by the captivity of Jerusalem, which is in Sepharad according to Obadiah 1: 20. Here Spinoza a Jew born in Amsterdam in 1932 was an outspoken defender of freedom, tolerance and moderation. And so when Johan de Witt, the great liberal statesman of the Dutch Republic, whose political motto was "true freedom" was lynched by a mob whipped into a frenzy by reactionary instigators tacitly or silently without words was backed by orthodox Calvinist clerics, Spinoza wanted to rush onto the scene and place a sign that read (in Latin): "The lowest of barbarians." If his landlord had not held him back, the gentle philosopher would surely have been lynched himself by this mob. Here is a conflict where the unjust are an abomination to the just and the upright in the way is an abomination to the wicked according to Proverbs 29: 27.

Spinoza suffered much for his lifelong dedication to the freedom of thought and expression. His view that God did not create the world and his disbelief in miracles and the immortality of the soul so enraged the rabbis of his Sephardic synagogue in Amsterdam that he was banished from the Jewish community for life at the age of 23. Here those who believe in freedom here refuse to suffer for Christ and so they suffer not only from their own kind but from at the hands of the wicked because they may not believe in Christ and mock at the fact that sin is a reality in our world and that he would be like a false witness that has a disbelief in the miracles of Christ and the disbelief of the immortality of the soul according to Proverbs 14: 5, 6, 7, 8 , 9, 10, 11, 12.

Spinoza suffered much for his long-life dedication to the freedom of thought and expression. His view that God did not create the world, and his disbelief in miracles and the immortality of the soul so enraged the rabbi of his Sephardic synagogue in Amsterdam that he was banished from the Jewish community for life at the age of 23. Only one of his books about the French philosopher Descartes, could be published under his own name during his life time. Here Ian Buruma in this Guest Essay of his --- claims that there were other great thinkers in the 17th century such as Thomas Hobbes and Gottfried Wihelm Leibniz who prepared the ground for enlightenment of the 18th century. But few still appeal as much to our imagination as Spinoza does. In these times, his radical advocacy of freedom still seems urgent. This is perhaps why new books about him are coming out all the time including Jonathon Israel's 2023 magnum opus "Spinoza, life and legacy," Steven Nadler's "Think least of Death: Spinoza how to live and die." And even a novel, "The Spinoza problem" by the psychiatrist Irvin Yalom. And all that for a philosopher by Christians and Jews as the devil's disciple long after his own time. Spinoza was convinced that all people were imbued with the capacity to reason and that we should seek the truth about the world we live in. Spinoza can be considered as an atheist like psychiatrist Irvin Yalom who is as an atheist and existential psychiatrist from Stanford University, and therefore an incredible resource for the secular community when it comes to facing existential dread in our world.

Spinoza was convinced that all people were imbued with the capacity to reason and that we should seek the truth about the world we live in. He insisted that our rational faculties could provide us with a path toward a better life and better politics. He wrote in an essay, "True philosophy is the discovery of the "true good" and without knowledge of the good human happiness is impossible." The true good, in Spinoza's view can be found only through reason. But this reasoning is feigned love in God and the unequal doctrine that Spinoza believes in. And loving humanity and not God when in reality we should be equal in believing things that are equal by not having love for one thing and hating or disbelieving in God. When God made himself equal to man by creating man in his own image. And we know that man is also not equal with God because of his omnipotent power that here Spinoza goes totally against the Authorized King James Version Bible establishing his own righteousness and being unequal in his doctrines of righteousness and Spinoza claiming he is not into adultery and whoredom when these sins of his unbelief of refusing to acknowledge the miracles and resurrection and the immortality in the Bible are worse than those who have committed whoredom and adultery according to Romans 10: 3 and Jeremiah 3: 9, 10, 11, 12, 13 and Psalms 17: 1, 2. Here if you are guilty of one sin you are guilty of all sins according to James 2: 10. Even if you have not committed all the listed sins in the Bible except only one you are guilty of all sins. Because Christ went to the cross for all the sins that mankind has been born into and man is in need of salvation because of sin. Here a haughty approach to not believing something because people may think you are crazy or be considered a psychiatric case is not humility in the sight of God and therefore in the long run you will not reap the rewards of honour but only destruction in the end according to Proverbs 18: 12. This sums up my argument of Ian Buruma Guest Essay in the New York Times dated March 2nd / 2024 and March 3rd / 2024 since I have made my point here and continuing on would only be redundant I will now conclude here by saying that if Spinoza has sought the truth he would have not declared that he believed that God did not create the world and that the miracles and the resurrection and immortality were not true or did not exist in reality. But those like Spinoza who have this mindset will eventually become ashamed of their beliefs that put them in a spotlight of shame according to Daniel 12: 2, 3.

For if you don't believe in miracles and immortality and the crucifixion and death and resurrection of Jesus Christ and you do not have an open mind for believing that miracles and immortality exists in the realm of common sense and reasoning. Then at least take for instance the existence of immortality that is eternal and how the resurrection is possible to bring us into that immortality. For if God has the power to resurrect a human being into immortality who God who has existed for as long as existence itself. Why do some of us deny immortality and miracles? As an example if a person would tell you in the 12th or 13th century that we are able to build a TV or build a computer or build a car the runs about at maximum speed of an excess of 200 miles an hour in a few seconds down a quarter mile track --- they would say they don't believe it is possible and they would consider you to be a psychiatric case much like we who believe in the resurrection today. And today are we are considered to be a nut or a religious fanatic because of our belief in the resurrection. Therefore, we are accused of being a religious fanatic or a nut. So, this is haughty reasoning that spawn's humiliation.

CHAPTER 9
Power of Humiliation

Humiliation is a powerful condition of the human spirit, since it reduces a person to a lower position in one's own eyes to a state of mortification. That may cause a person to rebel or lash out at those near or around them. And those humiliated may take this rage out on strangers as well. One Example of this rage is 5,500 children that have been killed since the October 7th / 2023 Israeli attacks according to Palestinian officials. That is one Palestinian child killed every 10 minutes, or about out of every 200 children in the Gaza Strip.

It came at a time of World's Children's Day Celebrated annually on November 20th which is a global initiative promoting children's rights, safety, education, health and happiness. It came amid Israel's war on Gaza. About half of Gaza's population of 2.3 million people are children. An additional 1,800 children are missing under the rubble, most of them presumed dead. A further 9,000 children have been injured, many with life changing consequences. Many of these children have lived through the trauma of multiple wars. The infographic here lists the names and ages (Too many names and children to list) of less than half of those children killed:

Israeli attacks have killed at least 5,500 children since October 7th / 2023
0 years old to 17 years old.
That is one Palestinian child killed every 10 minutes.
An additional 1,800 children are still missing under the rubble, most of them presumed dead.
A further 9,000 children have been injured, many with life-changing consequences.
Many children have lived through the trauma of multiple wars.
Gaza is becoming a graveyard for children.

And the numbers of these children are only half of the children killed. And so, at the time of this writing many more will be killed now and in the future before there is any end in sight for this war.

Here it comes as no surprise since God has now possibly given man a serious burden of trauma the same way Christ was traumatized and then crucified and how we rejected Christ where judgment came to us all by having man's sons and daughters or children killed in this war that came near or about November 20th according to Jeremiah 16: 1, 2, 3, 4, 5, 6, 7, 8, 9, 10, 11, 12, 13, which is World's Children's day celebrated annually on this November 20th day.

Also these mass shootings we have now experienced in our communities for years since terrorism became a serious problem in the early 1970's for instance --- is also one example of a person who has been given the psychological power to kill on a mass scale by the power of being humiliated as being a lone wolf or outcast in society. And so therefore humiliation is a powerful assaultive aspect and agent that is extremely dangerous in the hands of a person; like a country's leader or known as a dictator or tyrant.

Here Donald Trump and his international colleague Vladimir Putin are now considered at the time of this writing on March 19th / 2024 as two political adversaries of our just politicians in our world who despise their ongoing atrocities and abusive rhetoric that has bonded Putin and Trump into a company of worldwide dictators; because that is all they have left. Statements from Trump like Trump says quote: "If I don't get elected, there is going to be a bloodbath" as mentioned on CNN on March 18 / 2024. And how he boasts that this close relationship we know that he has with Putin that Trump says quote "I can prevent World War III very easily". These kind of statements and the fact of this so called "bloodbath" is a threat to our fragile peaceful condition that we have now after these wars in Ukraine and Israel; is that here violence is in the midst of not only Donald Trump but anyone associated with him according to Ezekiel 28: 16. Here by peace he shall destroy many innocent human lives because of this power of humiliation and his haughty character that spawns this violent rhetoric in his comments to the media according to Daniel 8: 24, 25.

How is he to destroy many innocent lives? There is what you would call a peaceful approach to genocide in order to save the world we live in at the expense of many lives being shattered because of murderous atrocities brought to these lives forming this convincing propaganda that is being produced by the deliberate depletion of the worldwide economy and because of these wars in Ukraine and Israel and the suffering of these wars and so this propaganda is to compel the world to submit to a one world Government of the Antichrist or Beast of Revelation 17: 12, 13. That is if they accept a leader like Donald Trump as he has said that he could bring on a bloodbath if he is not elected. Or he said if he is elected, he could easily prevent World War III from happening, would certainly convince the world to be safely preserved from violence and war. Here the notion that Trump is clamping down on these issues would be considered false and misleading statements.

The number and scale of Trump's statements in public speeches, remarks and tweets identified as false by scholars, fact checkers, and commentators were characterized as unprecedented for an American president and unprecedented in U.S. politics. The New Yorker called falsehoods a distinctive part of his political identity, and they have also been described by Republican political advisor Amanda Carpenter as a gaslighting tactic. His White House had dismissed the idea of objective truth or objective in a sense of coming from the mind and not from outside sources. So, his campaigns and presidency have been described as being post truth and hyper- Orwellian. Here Orwellian is an adjective describing a situation, idea, or societal condition that George Orwell identified as being destructive to the welfare of a free and open society. It denotes an attitude and brutal policy of draconian or cruel control by propaganda, surveillance, disinformation, denial of truth and doublethink which is a process of indoctrination in which subjects are expected to simultaneously accept two conflicting beliefs as truth, often at odds with their own memory or sense of reality. Here doublethink is related to, but differs from hypocrisy.

Also, the manipulation of the past, including the unperson --- a person whose past existence is expunged from the public record and memory, practiced by modern repressive governments. Often this includes the circumstances depicted in his novels, particularly "Nineteen Eighty-Four", despite the narrative depicting society in which only governmental employees are under repressive scrutiny, but political doublespeak (Doublespeak is language that deliberately obscures, disguises, distorts, or reverses the meaning of words) is criticized throughout his work such as "Politics and the English Language" The term "Orwellian" is the most widely used adjective derived from the name of a modern writer.

Trump's rhetorical signature included disregarding data from federal institutions that was incompatible to his arguments; quoting hearsay, anecdotal evidence or unpublished evidence, and questionable claims in partisan media or firm adherence to a party, faction, cause or person especially one who is exhibiting blind, prejudiced and unreasoning allegiance as mentioned in the media, denying reality (including his own statements) and distracting when falsehoods were exposed.

During the first year of Trump's presidency, The Washington Post's fact checking team wrote that Trump was "the most fact-challenged politician "it had" ever encountered... the pace and volume of the president's misstatements means that we cannot possibly keep up." The Post found that as president, Trump made more than 30,000 false or misleading claims, increasing from an average of a six a day in his first year as president to 39 claims a day in his final year. The most common false or misleading claims by Trump involved the economy and jobs, his border wall proposal and his tax legislation. He had also made false statements regarding prior administrations as well as other topics, including crime, terrorism, immigration, Russia and the Mueller probe, the Ukraine probe, immigration and the COVID 19 pandemic. Senior Administration officials had also regularly given false, misleading or tortured statements to the news media, which made it difficult for the news media to take official statements seriously. Here Trump and those who support him because of being so haughty in spirit that they are blinded by the fact the they think they can lie their way through life and prosperity, but that is not so if you are going to give tortured and misleading statements to the news media. Scorning just men or reporters or journalists in the news media or news media personnel who are up and coming in the news media as reporters and journalists according to Isaiah 28: 14, 15, 16, 17, 18. And these lies have brought on death and the slain in the city of politicians who are rejecting the prophetic warnings of the Authorized King James Version Bible. And both these are wars on going in Ukraine and Israel and their tanks rattling their wheels in war according to Nahum 3: 1, 2, 3, 4, 5, 6.

Trump and Putin and their haughty behaviour is a result or their humiliation in the media for their injustices they have caused like the lies brought on by Trump and his support of a dictator like Putin who has had thousands of civilians and soldiers slaughtered while he relishes in leadership in the country of Russia. Is there a positive indirectly speaking here of the "Power of humiliation?" Has ISIS been criticized and humiliated because of their terrorist acts? Unlike that terrorists act done against Moscow on March 22 / 2024 at Crocus City hall? An entertainment complex on the out skirts of Russia's Capital Moscow, where a rock concert by the group "Picnic" was about to take place? Was this terrorist act a power of humiliation? Video showed at least four people opening fire in the building's foyer before entering the hall itself and continuing to shoot. Russian authorities said the attackers then set fire to the hall using flammable liquid. Despite helicopters dropping water over the building, it took 10 hours to extinguish the flames.

Has ISIS been humiliated because of their terrorist acts in the past? Has this given them the power to commit a massive and surprising attack against Putin's Moscow in Russia putting Putin in his place for Putin being a liar by claiming allegiance with all the terrorists and dictator organizations and countries around the world in order to receive worldwide support from terrorists and from his humiliating atrocities he has committed on his own people and the atrocities committed in Ukraine and influencing the war in Israel trying to in vain compliment and mimic terrorists who are brilliant war makers and negotiators?

Here Putin and the people in Russia have corrupted themselves to the point that supporting a man like Putin would benefit them greatly on a financial level for the access and possessions of commodities through accepting bribes from Putin's government. Here R.W. Carmichael former intelligence Analyst at U.S. Air Force (1962- 1970) Says the following:

"Also, I am going to give you a very different answer than most. And that is that the Russian people don't rise up against Putin and his corruption because, in one way or another, they are almost all involved in it.

The corruption is not just at the top. It is pervasive throughout the population and culture and has been that way for over one hundred years without a pause. It isn't just the oligarchs who are corrupt. The traffic cop that stops you wants a bribe. The checker at the supermarket can sell you stuff that "fell off the truck." The black market has everything, but at far higher prices. Slots in good tertiary or third rank of importance in education are bought with bribes. Military officers are promoted on the basis of bribes and connections, not competence. It is just pervasive from top to bottom.

The best way I know if to get a good understanding of how bad it is, --- is a television show by President Zelenskyy of Ukraine called "Servant of the people." This was the number one TV show in both Russia and the Ukraine for good reason. And it is basically why he was elected President.

In the series Zelenskyy plays a high school history teacher who is videoed by a student during a rant about corruption in the Ukraine. The video is posted online and goes viral and he is elected President of the Ukraine.

But corruption is far more pervasive and resistant to repair than he imagined. Indeed, the military and government are corrupt. And there are the oligarchs. And the petty swindlers. And even his own family is taking bribes. And these are difficult to change. It seems that everyone he meets is corrupt. and the solutions are few and far between.

This TV series is why Zelenskyy was elected and not some Vague CIA plot as Putin claims. The Ukrainian people felt that Zelenskyy could clearly see the corruption and would call it out. Any they had which was a very good idea of what approaches he might take to correct the problems." --- Unquote.

Here shortly before Trump secured the 2016 Republican nomination, The New York Times reported "that legal experts across the political spectrum say "Trump's Rhetoric reflected" a constitutional worldview that shows contempt for the First Amendment, the separation of powers and the rule of law "adding" many conservative and libertarian legal scholars warn that electing Mr. Trump is a recipe for a constitutional crisis." Political scientists warned that candidate Trump's rhetoric and actions mimicked those of other politicians who ultimately turned authoritarian once in office. Some scholars have concluded that during Trump's tenure or during the holding of the presidential office and largely due to his actions and rhetoric, the U.S. has experienced democratic backsliding. Many prominent Republicans have expressed similar concerns that Trump's perceived disregard for the rule of law betrayed conservative principles.

During the first two years of his presidency, Trump Repeatedly sought to influence the Department of Justice to investigate Clinton, the Democratic National Committee, and Comey. He persistently repeated a variety of allegations, at least some of which had already been investigated or debunked. In spring 2018, Trump told white house counsel Don McGahn he wanted to order the Department of Justice to prosecute Clinton and Comey, but McGahn advised Trump such action would constitute abuse of power and invite possible impeachment. In May 2018, Trump demanded that the Department of Justice investigate "whether or not the FBI or the DOJ infiltrated or surveyed the Trump Campaign for Political Purposes," which the Department of Justice referred to its inspector general. Although, it is not unlawful for a president to exert influence to the Department of Justice to open an investigation, presidents have avoided to doing so to prevent perceptions of political interference by having assiduously or have persisted attention to application in order to cunningly avoid to doing so in order to prevent these perceptions of political interference.

Sessions resisted several demands by Trump and his allies for investigations of political opponents, causing Trump to repeatedly express frustration, saying at one point, "I don't have an attorney general." While criticizing the special counsel investigation in July 2019. Trump falsely claimed that the Constitution ensures that "I have to the right to do whatever I want as president." Trump had on multiple occasions either suggested or promoted views of extending his presidency beyond normal limits similarly to that presidency that Putin is gladly subject to in Russia.

Trump Frequently criticized the independence of the judiciary for unfairly interfering in his administration's ability to decide policy. In November 2018, in an extraordinary rebuke of a sitting president, Roberts criticized Trump's characterization of a judge who had ruled against his policies as an "Obama judge," adding "That's not law." In October 2020, twenty Republican former U.S. attorneys among them appointees by each Republican president since Eisenhower, characterized Trump as "a threat to the rule of law in our country." Here his haughty character is a threat and he would bring on destructive measures if given the authority of absolute power. Greg Bower, who worked in the Trump Administration, asserted, "It's clear that president Trump views the Justice Department and the FBI as his own personal law firm and investigative agency, much like the "Kremlin" that Putin associates with in Russia. Here the name "Kremlin" means, "fortress inside a city" and is often used as metonymically to refer to the Russian government. It previously referred to the government of the Soviet Union (1922 - 1991) and its leaders. Metonymically refers to a figure of speech consisting of the use of the name of one thing for that of another of which is an attribute or with which it is associated (as crown in "lands" belonging to the crown). Here it appears that this word was always associated with absolute control in government in Russia. Here it is a "citadel" or a stronghold in governing a city or a country.

Also, Trump dismissed FBI Director on May 9th / 2017, saying he had accepted the recommendations of Attorney General Sessions and Deputy Attorney General Rod Rosenstein to dismiss Comey. Session's recommendation was based on Rosenstein, while Rosenstein wrote that Comey should be dismissed for his handling of the conclusion of the FBI investigation into the Hillary Clinton email controversy. On May 10th, Trump met Russian Foreign Minister Sergey Lavrov and Russian Ambassador Sergey Kishlak. Based on White House notes of the meeting, Trump told the Russians, "I just fired the head of FBI. He was crazy, a real nut job... I faced great pressure because of Russia. That's taken off."

On May 11th Trump said in a videoed interview... "Regardless of recommendation, I was going to fire Comey... in fact, when I decided to just do it, I said to myself, I said, you know, this Russia thing with Trump and Russia is a made-up story." Such haughtiness and boasting coming from Trump here.

On May 18, Rosenstein told members of the U.S. Senate that he recommended Comey's dismissal while knowing Trump had already decided to fire Comey. In the aftermath of Comey's firing, the events were compared with those of the Saturday Night Massacre during Richard Nixon's administration where this Saturday Night massacre was a series of events that took place in the United States on the evening of Saturday, October 20th / 1973, during the Watergate scandal.

U.S. president Richard Nixon ordered General Elliot Richardson to fire Special Prosecutor Archibald Cox; Richardson refused and resigned effective immediately. Nixon then ordered Deputy Attorney General William Ruckelshaus to fire Cox; Ruckelshaus refused and also resigned. Nixon then order the third most - senior official at the Justice Department Solicitor General Robert Bork, to fire Cox. Bork carried out the dismissal as Nixon asked. Bork stated that he intended to resign afterward but was persuaded by Richardson and Ruckelshaus to stay on for the good of the Justice Department. And so here there was debate over whether Trump had provoked a constitutional crisis, as he had dismissed the man leading an investigation into Trump's associates. Trump's statements raised concerns of potential obstruction of justice. In Comey's memo about a February 2017 meeting with Trump, Comey said Trump attempted to persuade him to abort the investigation into Flynn.

Early into his presidency, Trump developed a highly contentious relationship with the news media, repeatedly referring to them as "the fake news media and the enemy of the people." As a candidate, Trump had refused press credentials for offending publications but said he would not do so if elected. Trump both privately and publicly mused about taking away critical reporters' White House press credentials. At the same time the Trump White House gave temporary press passes to far-right pro-Trump fringe outlets, such as "InfoWars" and "The Gateway Pundit," which are known for publishing hoaxes and conspiracy theories.

On his first day in office, Trump falsely accused journalists of understating the size of the crowd at his inauguration and called the news media "among the most dishonest human beings on earth." Trump's claims were notably defended by Press Secretary Sean Spicer, who claimed the inauguration crowd had been the biggest in history, a claim disproven by photographs. Trump's senior advisor Kellyanne Conway then defended Spicer when asked about falsehood, saying it was an alternative fact, not a falsehood.

The administration frequently sought to punish and blocked access for reporters that broke stories about the administration. Trump frequently criticized right-wing media outlet Fox News for being insufficiently supportive of him, threatening to lend his support for alternatives to Fox News on the right. On August 16 / 2018, the Senate unanimously passed a resolution affirming that "the press is not the enemy of the people".

The relationship between Trump, the news media, and fake news has been studied. One study found that between October 7th and November 14th / 2016, while one in four Americans visited a fake news website, Trump supporters visited the most fake news websites, which were over whelming pro-Trump and "almost 6 in 10 visits to fake news websites came from the 10% of people with the most conservative online information diets." Brendan Nyhan one of the authors of the study, said in an interview, "people got vastly more misinformation from Donald Trump than they did from fake news websites."

In October / 2018, Trump praised U.S. Representative Greg Gianforte for assaulting political reporter Ben Jacobs in 2017. According to analysts, the incident marked the first time the president has openly and directly praised a violent act against a journalist on American soil. "Later that month as CNN and prominent Democrats were targeted with mail bombs, Trump initially condemned the bomb attempts but shortly thereafter blamed the "Mainstream Media that I refer to as fake News " for causing a very big part of the anger we see today in our society."

The Trump Justice Department obtained by court order the 2017 phone logs or email metadata of reporters from CNN., The New York Times, The Washington Post, Buzzfeed and Politico as part of investigations into leaks of classified information. Here the power of humiliation is at work making Trump who is now possibly humiliated because of his lack of integrity and his outright lies may have ordered these investigations of classified information to conceal whatever did not get out into the public. Since if this information ever got out like the possible conspiracy to burn alive in a furnace a servant of God or have some sort of political connections with other authoritarian figures around the world like perhaps cruel dictators like Putin that it would cause a humiliating shadow to be cast upon Donald Trump causing that power of humiliation to provoke Donald Trump to politically run amok in his presidency of the United States. Like Trump has said that if he doesn't get elected there is going to be a bloodbath as was mentioned on CNN News on March 18th / 2024. This is indeed an eerie omen and premonition of what is about to occur.

Here also Donald Trump has said or was mentioned on CNN news on March 20 / 2024 that any Jewish person who votes for democrats hates their religion and hates the state of Israel. Quite a contradictory statement since Donald Trump supports Vladimir Putin who influenced the war in Israel. Also 42-year-old Republican Senator Katie Britt of Alabama had made a speech after Biden's State of the Union address on March 7th / 2024 at 11 p.m. She wore the color green for hope, and the salvation of Christ. Here she is deceived here into doing this speech in order to support Donald Trump here. So, it is a fight politically between good and evil. The evil wants to save themselves and live by relying on Donald Trump on possibly ending the wars in Ukraine and Israel if he were elected as U.S. president for the second time and therefore ending the Middle East crisis. Also here Senator Katie Britt of Alabama being a Republican believes in Donald Trump and how both are trying to establish their own righteousness by trying to bring peace into a sinful infested world and rejecting the true servants of God and the true followers of Christ who would be the ones to bring in true peace to the world as Donald Trump and Katie Britt rejects these true servants and followers of Christ and trying to establish their own righteousness with money instead of a Barter System in this world where the root of all evil is money according to Romans 10: 3 and 1st Timothy 6: 8, 9, 10, 11, 12.

Here also there would be a servant of God that would be a scapegoat for the controversy of the books he has written and because of these books that has influenced world government sedition, that it will bring on worldwide perdition of civilization. So the outcome would be a trial by fire in a furnace as a sentence for perdition of civilization done to a servant of God that is also arranged and done by a covenant between the worldwide Magistrates of the God of the Authorized King James Version Bible and the worldwide Magistrates of the Antichrist according to 1st Peter 1: 7. And here it would surprise the whole world of Babylon if this servant of God was delivered by God alive out of that burning fiery furnace according to Jeremiah 51: 41.

Also, this situation of a furnace judgment by this Antichrist who could be Donald Trump and his right-hand man Vladimir Putin could also be brought on by the power of humiliation by the power of humiliation of this sexual assault and harassment and defamation lawsuit of 83.3 million dollars brought against Donald Trump by E Jean Carroll. A writer who was female who had experienced this sexual assault and harassment and defamation at the hands of Donald Trump. And who this female writer E Jean Carroll had also prevailed in this lawsuit of 83.3 million dollars.

Also, here Donald Trump tries to make it appear like he is a reliable politician by using the selling of merchandise like selling Bible's titled "God Bless the U.S.A. Bibles" for 60 dollars each. Trump is also selling "Fragrance" and "Never Surrender Shoes" and was also selling T-Shirts with his mug shot on them in order to raise funds since he has been in court being subject to a series of lawsuits and being up on charges for his unlawful allegations brought against him regarding possible sexual assaults and the violence of January 6th / 2021 for the insurrection at the U.S. Capitol building. With more than 1,033 people have been arrested for storming the Capitol Hill building on January 6th / 2021, with charges ranging from obstruction of an official proceeding to assault.

But 28 months after the attempted insurrection, a significant number of rioters are still awaiting their sentencing as of May /2023. And around 47 % of those arrested - 485 individuals have received criminal sentences, while the rest are waiting for their trials or haven't yet reached plea agreements. According to the U.S. Attorney's Office for the District of Columbia, 277 defendants were sentenced to periods of incarceration, with longer prison terms for those who engaged in violence or threats. So far, the median prison sentence for the January 6th / 2021 rioters is 60 days according to TIME's calculation of the public records. An additional 113 rioters have been sentenced to periods of home detention, while most sentences have included fines, community service and probation for low level offenses like illegally parading or demonstrating in the Capitol, which is a misdemeanor. Here it is obvious that this scripture here fulfills this Biblical prophecy of this event or is a partial fulfillment; since who knows if more violence will happen in the midst of Donald Trump's presence as a presidential candidate or as a former U.S. president or possibly becoming a U.S. president for the second time in November 2024 according to Ezekiel 28: 16.

The longest sentence given to anyone charged in the January 6th riot to date went to far-right Oath Keepers founder Stewart Rhodes, who was sentenced on May 25 / 2023 to 18 years in prison after being convicted of seditious conspiracy for his role in helping orchestrate the pro-Trump attack on the Capital. Prosecutors said that Rhodes, 58, was the mastermind behind a plot to keep Trump in power after he lost the 2020 election, marshaling dozens of followers across the country to descend on Washington on Jan 6th. During an eight-week trial last fall, prosecutors revealed thousands of messages between Rhodes and other members of the Oath Keepers, an anti-government militia group, in advance of the Capitol attack, including one where Rhodes told his followers to prepare their mind, body, spirit for "civil war." Rhodes and his followers converged on the Capitol after assembling an arsenal of weapons and setting up "quick reaction force" teams at a Virginia hotel that could deploy guns into the nation's capitol if needed to support their plot, according to court documents.

You sir, present an ongoing threat and a peril to this country, to the republic and to the very fabric of our democracy. said U.S. District Court Judge Amit Mehta during Rhodes' sentencing. A Yale Law graduate and military veteran, Rhodes is the first member of the January 6th mob to be convicted of seditious conspiracy, a rarely used charge for when two or more people conspire to "overthrow, put down or to destroy by force" the U.S. Government to bring war against it. The charge can also be brought against people who plot to use force to oppose the authority of the government or to block the execution of a law. Judge Mehta agreed with prosecutors to classify his crimes as an act of terrorism against the government, a categorization that sharply increased his ultimate sentence. Here "sedition" is prohibited by the Authorized King James Version Bible according to Galatians 5: 19, 20, 21.

Here Rhodes also has a patch on his left eye where he may have suffered damage to his left eye as a military war veteran. Also as I have mentioned in my second book "Open Tomb, Aviation 666, and Monsters of Genesis" that my left eye's vision was also damaged by psychiatric drug called "Haldol" that had only damaged my left eye's optic nerve and only distorted my vision but was not blinded that was administered by psychiatrist Dr. Georgia Walton from CAMH psychiatric institution where I was incarcerated in. Here she sent me to optometrists Dr. Dang and Dr. Chu at a clinic that was at 1008 King St. West in Toronto, Ontario, Canada. Either it was Dr. Dang or Dr. Chu who did my eye examine because the optometrist who did my eye examine did not give me his name. Who was either Dr. Dang or Dr. Chu who did my eye examine who had deliberately shun the diagnostic light in my eye for a prolong period of time to deliberately blind my left eye after using a lot of eye drops to dilate my pupils. By possibly claiming that I must have looked at the sun too long in order to vindicate Dr. Walton in court of law from a possible lawsuit that I may have filed against her. Here Dr. Walton did not want to possibly face a lawsuit. Because at the time that she wanted to administer the medication to me that I had refused, --- was because I was incompetent or not capable to consent to my own treatment at the time. So, she then forced this medication called "Haldol" on me with security guards present at her orders to give this medication by injection. Where here me being incompetent or not capable to consent to my own treatment I would have had a good case against her to sue her in a court of law.

Here my left eye is now blind or severely darkened and is now considered a single eye according to Matthew 6: 22; and that it was the chastisement of a cruel one by blinding my left eye and it was the wound of an enemy; which this wound is permanent blindness where there is no one to help my cause of this blind left eye now. So, there is no one to plead my cause because it is hard to prove that my retina was damaged deliberately by this optometrist since a psychiatric patient is not credible to bring a lawsuit against a qualified psychiatrist like Dr. Georgia Walton and a qualified optometrist like Dr. Dang or Dr. Chu. And there also are no healing medicines because you cannot heal a retina of the eye once it is damaged and detached from the back of the interior of the eyeball according to Jeremiah 30: 12, 13, 14, 15, 16, 17.

Also Donald Trump's right eye as mentioned online, is that his right eye is dim or has dark vision according to Zechariah 11: 17. And it could be considered as evil; since seeing clearly through your left eye left is considered to be on the side of evil according to Matthew 6: 23 and Matthew 25: 33, 41. Here it is true that no prophecy of the scripture is of any private interpretation according to 2nd Peter 1: 20. Having said this, will I burn in that furnace since Steward Rhodes' left eye is also blind or damaged ? You see God likes to spook his servants by leaving these road markers of discouragement to give humanity the benefit of the doubt and not only for me and those who are truly faithful to the Authorized King James Version Bible, but for Donald Trump and his followers. Here God has no respect of persons when it comes to knowing what the truth is according to Colossians 3: 25. Because the truth according to the Bible is based solely and purely on faith. I am not spooked by this damaged or blinded left eye that Steward Rhodes has because if I burn, I have already surrendered to God's chastisement and will be delivered from hell after I get burned alive to death according to 1st Corinthians 11: 31, 32 and Matthew 10: 28.

Here Christ was also in poverty when he was crucified. But because of his crucifixion and death he did not prosper. But his blood may deliver me from poverty and the crucifixion of that furnace. Also, if I do get delivered from this furnace, I may end up taking a "spoil" and take the monetary assets and real estate or treasures from those who sentence me to that furnace. And devour them on a financial level as well as leading them through this pillage and death by most of the worldwide magistrates who will sentence my enemies like Donald Trump and Vladimir Putin and possibly other dictators who they have close relations with, after being delivered from this furnace and taking this "spoil" perhaps in the billions of dollars and with Christ and with them who are faithful to him and we may take over the government of the Anti-Christ and with our Lord Jesus Christ and we or us who are the true Christians of the Authorized King James Version Bible will take over with billions of dollars that has been pillaged from Donald Trump and Vladimir Putin. And sending them to be devoured by a furnace sentence.

And also us true Christians of the Authorized King James Version Bible who are not only the Democrats of the world but who are some, or most Republicans of the world too where I will --- being delivered from this furnace in order to have these billions of dollars for these Democrats and some of these Republicans to get us all to launch the plans and incremental steps to beginning to implement the Barter System worldwide. In order to eliminate money currencies in the world in the days of these Kings of the Anti- Christ who will turn to the God of the Authorized King James Version Bible according to Daniel 7: 12, 13, 14, 15, 16, 17, 18, 19, 20, 21, 22, 23, 24, 25, 26, 27 and in the days of the Kings of the God of the Authorized King James Version Bible where this furnace Judgment will take place just before or during or just after Armageddon according to Jeremiah 15: 13,

14, 21 and Hebrews 10: 27 and Daniel 7: 10, 11 and Daniel 2: 44, 45 and 1st Timothy 6: 6, 7, 8, 9, 10, 11, 12, 13, 14, 15, 16, 17, 18, 19 , 20, 21. Here regarding our fate in this world is of either accepting Christ now and either pay now or pay later with having a non- democratic world and an emerging Antichrist and a One World Government that will bring on a temporary peace in the beginning according to 1st Thessalonians 5: 3 and which will lead to the genocide of true Christians and their converts. And eventually bring on Armageddon and the Mark of the Beast which is this one world digital currency implemented on humanity by conquest. In order to swear allegiance to Donald Trump and this One World Government of the Antichrist or Beast and this Mark of the Beast that will be possibly devised by Donald Trump to eliminate the economic morass we are now sinking in.

And if anyone refuses this one world digital currency they will be executed in a courtroom or slain by the citizens who have taken this Mark of the Beast according to Ezekiel 9: 5, 6, 7, 8, 9, 10, 11, and who have sworn allegiance to Donald Trump who would eventually become the Antichrist. Or whosoever this Antichrist would be since no Prophecy of Scripture is of any private interpretation according to 2nd Peter 1: 20. And the eventual outcome of everything I just mentioned in this paragraph and also the deception of the Beast and the Papacy or the Pope who is known in the Bible as the false prophet according to Revelation 13: 15, 16, 17, 18 and Revelation 6: 9, 10, 11 and Revelation 20: 4 and Revelation 16: 13, 14, 15, 16. Here eventually Donald Trump or this Antichrist and his money and gold shall cause him to come to his end and none shall help him according to Daniel 11: 43, 44, 45.

Also, in this coming One World Government of the God of the Authorized King James Version Bible and if I am delivered from that furnace and that I may rule with Christ. That we will not judge peaceful sinners like those who are gay or those who have a different sexual orientation or different religious ideological concepts since it is not for us to judge man this way physically and spiritually but to leave it in the hands of our God Jehovah the Lord Jesus Christ. Here we would in this world judge cold blooded murderers and mass murderers who have killed on a large scale many people in mass shootings and to judge appropriately domestic violence and violence against women. Like beatings and rapes and murders on women and sexual deviants who prey on women and children. Or like the pedophiles who prey on children and to be dealt with a severe judgment in the courts in our One World Government of the God of the Authorized King James Version Bible and by our worldwide Magistrates of the God of the Authorized King James Version Bible according to Deuteronomy 11: 32.

CHAPTER 10
Humility Destroys Destruction

Here in this chapter called "Humility Destroys Destruction," the opposite of this is also true that being Haughty can destroy you as well. Take for instance John Lennon who was assassinated by Mark David Chapman. The Beatle's icon was murdered by Mark David Chapman on December 8th / 1980, in a death that shocked the world and continues to inspire grief, anger, and wonder.

Upon returning home from a recording studio with his wife Yoko Ono, Lennon was shot four times in the back with a revolver and rushed to hospital where he was pronounced dead at around 11 p.m. He was 40 years old. Chapman then aged 25, had traveled from Hawaii and had asked Lennon to sign his copy of his latest album, "Double Fantasy" earlier that day.

"I saw the photo where he signed the autograph. It was flashed on TV again and again," Ono went on to write to fans a month later in an ad she took out in a major newspaper across the U.S. "Somehow that photo was harder for me to look at than the death photo," she wrote. John was in a hurry that afternoon. He did not have to give his autograph, but he did, while the man watched him, the man who was to betray John later.

When police found Chapman, he was famously reading a copy of J. D. Salinger's classic novel, "The Catcher in the Rye." That is about the story of Holden Caulfield, a teenage boy expelled from his prep school and is wandering through New York City over a few days, struggling to come to terms with the complexities of growing up and the seeming phoniness of the adult world. Chapman was sentenced to life in prison.

Chapman, although a fan of Lennon, was upset by the Liverpool singer's views on God - he was particularly irked or annoyed by a famous Lennon quip, about the Beatles being "more popular than Jesus Christ" as well as the lyrics to later songs "Imagine" and "God."

Having recently had a religious conversion prior to his decision to kill the musician, religion and belief was the motive behind the murder.

Although he refused to talk to the press for years after his arrest, Chapman eventually supplied audiotaped interviews to journalist Jack Jones, who used them to write the 1992 investigative book "Let Me Take You Down: Inside the Mind of Mark David Chapman."

In the book, a sister of one of Chapman's friends Jan Reeves said that he was angry towards Lennon's claim about the band being more popular than Jesus Christ, claiming that it was blasphemy.

Chapman was also said to be highly influenced by the Book "John Lennon: One Day at a Time" by Anthony Fawcett, which explored Lennon's life in New York City. Chapman's wife Gloria is quoted as saying: he was angry that Lennon would preach love and peace, and yet have millions of dollars. Chapman later said " He told us to imagine no possessions and there he was, with millions of dollars and yachts and farm and country estates. laughing at people like me who had believed the lies and bought the records and built a big part of their lives around his music."

He was obsessed with the concept of anti- phoniness as agonized over by the fictional protagonist of " The Catcher in the Rye," Holden Caulfield. " Saying that he doesn't believe in Jesus Christ and things like that. At that point, my mind was going through a total blackness of anger and rage. So, I brought the Lennon book home, into this "The Catcher in the Rye" milieu (or where the physical or social setting in which something occurs or develops) where my mindset is Holden Caulfield and anti- phoniness" Chapman said in "Let Me Take You Down: Inside the Mind of Mark David Chapman."

Here John Lennon was Haughty which is the opposite of humility which eliminates or destroys destruction? Was it an indirect judgment of God to send Mark David Chapman to assassinate John Lennon because of his media blasphemy of claiming that the Beatles were more popular than Jesus Christ? Since if John Lennon had used humility instead of being haughty, he would not have been assassinated and would have not destroyed himself by this imminent assassination that led to his death according to Proverbs 18: 12.

Also, Vladimir Putin would have not been able to have invaded Ukraine and have started this war in Ukraine and to cause so much destruction in Ukraine and to also have influenced that war in Israel if the world was operating on the Barter System worldwide. Here, Putin would have not been able to accumulate just over 680 billion dollars from those resources in Russia; resources like gold, Petroleum, Aluminum, Coal, Gas, Nickel, Copper, Electricity, Hydropower, Iron, Nuclear power, Tin, and Uranium. Because money is the root of all evil according to 1st Timothy 6: 8, 9, 10. Here the Barter System would be based on trade and mandatory rations without money. Since in our world everything is based on accumulating funds without having no limit in the amount of funds you can accumulate. We also don't have Rations in most if not all countries. So, Putin can possess an unlimited number of weapons to wage his war on Ukraine and able to threaten the world like he has done just recently or as of this writing on April 6, 2024.

Being haughty and not having humility creates destruction. Those who refuse to accept the Barter System are obsessed with money and having the pride of accumulating enormous amounts of cash or revenue in their pockets or bank accounts to purchase items. They Like the idea of having the power to possess whatever they like without restraint.

Here the Barter System is based on rations and trade. Where do commodities come from? From only two main resources of both Agriculture and minerals. These two resources come from the ground or from our mining and farming. Here the only cost to obtain these resources is labour. Also, all industry takes a major role in converting these resources into commodities like clothes, vehicles, housing, shelters, storage facilities, warehouses, food, aircraft, medicines, hospitals and the medical equipment and their supplies etc.

In order to produce these commodities, we are now using money to buy labour. Where Labour should be bought by trade and not money. Because money eliminates the concept of having rations put in place. For if we use rations with having a monetary system then what is the point of accumulating large sums of money? Here accumulating large sums of money creates out of control inflation where those who have large sums of money have unlimited buying power and it puts a huge strain on the economy with supply and demand. Furthermore, those who collect interest from money accumulate money without having to work because of the amount of funds they have accumulated. They are the cause of inflation because supply and demand increases. Here some people don't work. Because they collect interest from their money; and in turn they don't work to help to produce commodities where here production of commodities here lacks and therefore commodities become in high demand therefore increasing prices on commodities.

Here the Stock Market would be history if we had a Barter System because the Stock Market operates on monetary values and different currencies. Also having the Barter System implemented worldwide would eliminate different currencies that we now have in our world. Also, with the Barter System you would not need cash or money to buy items like furniture or a car or an airplane etc. because possessing power to obtain these commodities would be controlled by rations. And in time after the Barter System has been in place and operating for a while then prosperity would increase of being able to get more food or items. And inflation would be a thing of the past with this Barter System. Furthermore, if anyone does not show up for work in the Barter System they would be charged with fraud and go in front of a Judge for the reasons why he or she has not showed up for work. And if found guilty they could go to prison or jail for fraud.

Also, on March 26th / 2024 the Baltimore Key Bridge collapsed after a massive container ship lost power and crashed into the iconic Baltimore bridge, sending people and vehicles into the frigid Patapsco River. Unfortunately, our world has no rations to control that number of commodities that are sold and being distributed on a national or international scale. Had it been that our world would have had a Barter System with rations in place these frequent trips may have not even been necessary for these massive container ships. Therefore, avoiding the stress on those who work and operate these container ships and avoiding the mechanical stress by the wear and tear and hour by hour usage of these container ships 24 / 7. Here because of the lack of rations in buying commodities --- maintenance personnel and the operators for these ships are under extreme stress and must be on alert 24/7. It is a huge responsibility to operate these massive container ships where each journey of these massive container ships is in peril. My heart goes out to the men and women who must deal with the stress of doing these different jobs that require these commodities to be delivered on time by these massive container ships. Since here shipment depends on the maintenance and the operators of these massive container ships. Here anything can go wrong under the stress that these men and women endure each and every day and must run these ships to their destinations on time day in and day out. There is no room in this business to be haughty in your line of work; for if this is the case or being haughty by being overconfident is a recipe for disaster according to Proverbs 14: 16. Like what has happened here with the collision and collapse into the Francis Scott Key Bridge in Baltimore on March 26th / 2024. Humility brings us to a place of safety where we respect the prospect of dangerous outcomes that can possibly occur according to Proverbs 22: 4, 5. Nothing here is further from the truth.

The Barter System with rations would prevent those in power who are evil to climb the ladder to tyrannical leadership or become a brutal dictator like Putin has become. Because 680 billion dollars in the hands of a man like Vladimir Putin, is and can be a perilous outcome for the world. That is why a Barter System with rations implemented worldwide would prevent an evil leader or dictator from accumulating enormous amount of wealth and have the absolute barbaric control over their citizens by and of these tyrants who rule in these cruel dictatorships. This world and its atrocities especially the invasion and war in Ukraine and the war in Israel have been a thorn in the side of humanity just recently that has put a burden of psychological and economic stress on us all who love peace and have a love for humanity. I only hope that humanity finds some sort of solace in these problems we face today in our world.

Also, protests are another issue regarding the pride and haughtiness of man. Here humility has no part in a protest because it is all about how man likes to boastfully debate an issue whether it is a political issue or someone's unjust death. As an example, at least 11 Americans have been killed while participating in political demonstrations. And another 14 have died in other incidents linked to political unrest, according to data from non-profit monitoring political unrest in the United States. Nine of the people killed during protests were demonstrations taking part in Black Lives

Matter protests. Two were conservatives killed after pro-Trump "patriot rallies." All but one was killed by fellow citizens. The new data highlights the danger of the presence of guns during politically charged protests and raises concerns about continued violence during and after election day, when many Americans anticipate delays, confusion and protests before the winner of the presidential race is confirmed.

Most of the protesters killed were shot to death, and many of the incidents involved confrontations at protests that escalated and turned deadly when at least one of the people involved had a gun.

Lee Keltner, a navy veteran who made custom western hats, was shot after a "patriot rally" in Denver. Video and photographs of the incident appear to show Keltner slapping a security guard for a local news crew, who responds by pulling out a gun and shooting him. Aaron "Jay" Danielson, a far-right Trump supporter, was shot after a rally in Portland. Danielson's suspected killer, Michael Reinoehl, was a leftwing protester who called himself "anti-fascist", and who was later shot to death by law enforcement officials, an outcome Donald Trump referred to as retribution. Here Donald Trump has violence in his midst according to Ezekiel 28: 16.

Here protests lead to seditions and chaotic crowds that leads to injuries and murders or killings. Protests are indeed futile. And that to order or accomplish any positive results or outcomes at all in these protests or any protest at all that in the end, it indeed turns out negative. Can we change what is already and securely in place? Like government entities already elected and functioning In the structural alliances in the government that have also been associated in government along with their political members and their military members and their police and law enforcement members as well? Here haughty personalities clash with one another in an issue at a protest. Sedition here is prohibited by the Authorized King James Version Bible according to Galatians 5: 19, 20.

But humility brings peace and safety and destroys destruction. For there is no grace and peace in the proud and haughty, but humility brings that grace and peace in the end avoiding death and destruction. And where the results here of having humility affects the humble and subjects the humble to grace and peace according to 1st Peter 5: 5.

EPILOGUE

We are at a point in history where our world is experiencing violence and an increase in the rise of evil. That evil is not only the violence and atrocities we have experienced lately on a worldwide scale, but we have also experienced economic morass that we are now sinking in. With the problems of inflation ever further increasing, along with the increase of intense secularism in our world. Here that dictator known as the Beast or Antichrist or perhaps who is Donald Trump or his successor who becomes this Beast or Antichrist who will in the not- too- distant future if Donald Trump becomes president again in the U.S.; that he may very well during this presidency begin a religious revival to solve the world's problems during this upcoming presidency.

And how he would by propaganda solve the wars in Ukraine and Israel and bring peace to Ukraine and Israel and major portions of the Middle East and the other parts of the world. Where it will be a temporary and short-lived peace; that in the end it will bring total destruction according to 1st Thessalonians 5: 3.

This religious revival will win people to accept Donald Trump before and after he solves these middle east problems and the war in Israel and the war in Ukraine. After he succeeds in solving these problems he will be hailed as a hero and a savior to humanity. He will have this religious revival that will soon take place and will win a massive amount of people worldwide by a popular vote before and after he solves these problems like the war in Ukraine and the war in Israel and the economic morass that we are now sinking in.

Donald Trump or his successor (or whoever will become the Antichrist) will at this point use Artificial Intelligence and Robotics to make an image of himself and deceive the mass populace worldwide on planet earth. This robotic image will be fitted with Artificial Intelligence which will be connected by software to this one world digital currency and surveillance system in the form of a Biological Implant that will be a citizen's Global I.D. or mark on a person's body. He will then with this robotic image that is fitted with Artificial Intelligence control and keep track of 8 billion people on this planet regarding financial transactions and their medical records and their criminal activities and court dates and court appearances and court prosecutions and acquittals etc. and anyone who refuses this Global I.D. or Mark of The Beast, that they will then be brought in front of a judge. And there will be a law that will be legislated and implemented that will be mandatory to either take this Global citizenship I.D. which consists of a one world digital currency and surveillance system to keep track of 8 billion people on earth or if anyone who refuses this Global citizenship I.D. or Mark of the Beast and refuses to worship this robotic image of the beast should be killed or executed in a court of law according to Revelation 13: 14, 15, 16, 17, 18 and Revelation 20: 4. Also those who take this Mark of the Beast swearing allegiance to the Antichrist will hunt down those Christians and their converts who are refusing this Mark of the Beast according to Ezekiel 9: 5, 6, 7 and Ezekiel 13: 18, 19, 20.

There is another evil that is also secular in nature besides taking this Global citizenship I.D. known as the Mark of the Beast. Take for instance the eclipse of totality that has taken place on April 8th / 2024 in the region of Niagara Falls near Toronto, Ontario, Canada.

On April 8th / 2024 as the eclipse was taking place during its totality and since I am born again by drinking blood and water in order to receive the Holy Spirit, I experienced a burden in my body and spirit when the eclipse in its totality was taking place. I should have fasted on April 8th / 2024. And at the time I had also a psychiatric drug called "Invega" in my body. This psychiatric drug made me feel much worse during the totality of this eclipse after I ate on April 8th / 2024, the day of the eclipse where my body was defiled after eating and having this drug "Invega" in my body.

The reason I felt bad spiritually and physically? Was because I have the Holy Spirit in me. The eclipse is an evil event and the only reason it is evil is because it is considered an extremely secular event because most of the people in the world have rejected Christ and the Authorized King James Version Bible. So, the world celebrates eclipses on a secular level on a worldwide scale all around the world which makes this event that much more evil because they worship on a secular level a celestial body instead of the body of Christ.

Here I experienced this evil because my body is sown in weakness because of having the Holy Spirit in me and that's why when I don't fast, I feel this evil burden in my spirit and body during the eclipse. There is the glory of the celestial which is one --- and the glory of the terrestrial which is another. So, when I glory in the flesh as a terrestrial body by eating, I don't glory but suffer through the eclipse. And so only when I fast do I glory and not suffer through the eclipse as a terrestrial body.

Which is another type of glory that is either positive when I fast and not eat and not suffer through the eclipse or another type of glory that is negative when I eat and not fast by suffering through the eclipse. Those who are in the flesh and being not born again by not drinking blood and water by faith or are infidels of the Authorized King James Version Bible glory by eating and feeling good during the eclipse while eating during or before or after the eclipse according to 1st Corinthians 15: 39, 40, 41, 42, 43, 44, 45, 46 ,47, 48, 49, 50, and John 3: 6.

Here to worship the eclipse like CTV's Dan Riskin and Kelsey McEwen that were so obsessed by the eclipse that they were dancing. And that CTV's Adrian Ghobrial said on CP-24 news on April 9th / 2024 that the eclipse has come and gone, and that the world has not ended. People get the wrong idea that the eclipse is the immediate coming of the end of the world. When it is actually a sign that the prophetic events of the coming Antichrist one world government are near fulfillment and is about in a short period of imminent time of coming years bringing on those Antichrist one world government atrocities worldwide to pass according to Luke 21: 12, 13, 14, 15, 16, 17. And that this one world Government of the Antichrist is coming of not only in the Middle East and Europe but also in peaceful countries like Canada.

Here to also worship the eclipse and letting it save us by believing in it on a secular level and saying that it unites us all and is an event that we will never forget for the rest of our lives and saving the souvenirs that is a reminder of this eclipse and then rejecting Christ whom most people in this world have forsaken him is downright evil; and is where here Christ will also forsake us in the end and judge us. Since our time now is short on this planet because of the prophetic events that are now taking place. Since I would rather burn than to worship a moon going across the sun in an eclipse according to Isaiah 47: 13, 14, 15 and Luke 21: 8, 9, 10, 11, 12, 25, 26.

This eclipse is a sure sign of this coming one world government of the Antichrist or its near fulfillment that may or will take place in the coming next 10 to 30 years. Who are these political leaders like Donald Trump and Vladimir Putin? Who appear to have a Babylonian lifestyle. Here the term "Babylonian" refers according to the Merriam Webster's Collegiate Dictionary as "a city devoted to materialism and sensual pleasure." And which I have also have mentioned in this book that the term "Babylon" or "Babylonian" also refers to confusion. And also I am adding that it also refers to having the urge to possess and secure monetary funds and materialistic possessions like lavish cars and aircraft or airplanes and lavish clothes, food and similar everyday lavish items like computers, T.V.'s , Boats, snowmobiles and expensive real estate and possessing property in order to buy and selling it to make huge profits in the money and monetary world and further increasing these huge monetary finances they possess. And using these huge investments they have, by investing into the stock market as well.

Here what is my position as a sinner? Is that I am a sinner who is unable to govern as a world leader or help a world leader rule the planet. Since no one can take that office of Christ as a world leader according to Psalms 24: 1, 2, 3, 4, 5 ---- except it be given to him in the resurrection of immortality by receiving his salvation from our God. Since immortality is not subjected to sin according to 1st Corinthians 15: 53, 54, 55, 56, 57.

Here are these political leaders like Donald Trump and Vladimir Putin sinners? Since the Bible says yes as well to this question according to Romans 3: 9, 10, 11, 12, 23. Here the term "Babylon" refers to " Zerubbabel" and the term "Zerubbabel" or Babylon as I have mentioned in this book refers to confusion.

Here have I as a sinner been blamed or contemned for the war in Ukraine and Israel? And here I have also been condemned me as every "tree" or follower of our Lord Jesus Christ for following me for my written rhetoric regarding my revelations of the Biblical prophecies related to world events for writing these books and these emails and letters to and about celebrities and political entities in the high places and about Donald Trump and Vladimir Putin who both are now being labelled and related to Biblical prophecy? And about these violent events in our world that were prophesied like these stabbings and shootings and atrocities in our world related to these prophetic events mentioned in the Authorized King James Version Bible according to 2nd Timothy 3: 1, 2, 3, 4 ,5, 6, 7.

And the fact that the reason I was contemned or blamed for these wars and atrocities in Ukraine and Israel was because of revealing these Biblical prophetic events that have happened in our world as mentioned in the Authorized King James Version Bible. And for also smiting therefore upon my thigh or that I masturbated for not ever having a girlfriend since they who are infidels of the Authorized King James Version Bible considered me to be evil according Ezekiel 21: 9, 10, 11, 12, 13, 14, 15?

I am still a sinner according to the flesh where I was sealed by God by a cluster of light that went into my chest and while I was in the flesh, on Friday August 12th / 1983. And became born again by drinking the blood and water of Christ by faith to receive the Holy Spirit. Still after being born again I was still a sinner. Since I was not conceived by the Holy Ghost where God is not my biological Father like Christ had been when he was conceived in his mother's womb named Mary by the Holy Ghost. It is significant here to know that my biological mother's name was "Mary" as well. And that my biological father was a human on this planet where his semen was possibly inseminated into my biological mother by an extraterrestrial being or entity carrying out the divine plans of God as I have mentioned in detail in my book called "Open Tomb, Aviation 666, Monsters of Genesis." So here Christ was a deity or was God in the flesh, conceived by the Holy Ghost unlike us who were conceived by a biologically terrestrial father in the flesh on this planet.

Jesus Christ was conceived by the Holy Ghost --- since being conceived by the Holy ghost and born in the flesh that Christ was born without sin in the flesh and unlike us who are born in flesh with sin being these goats of sin. But some of us goats have turned from this sin to serve the living God and have become sheep being born again or trusting in God in the flesh according to Galatians 2: 20 instead. And this judgment of goats and sheep vary with the goats being judged in a negative way on the left by God and the sheep being judged in a positive way on the right according to Matthew 25: 32, 33, 34, 35, 36, 37, 38, 39, 40, 41, 42, 43, 44, 45, 46.

Here some of us goats will turn from sin and will turn to serve the living God in the flesh and being born again either in the flesh without drinking that blood and water or being born again by drinking that blood and water by faith in order to receive the Holy Spirit. Yet still being sinners in the flesh according to Romans 5: 10, 11, 12, 13, 14, 15, 16, 17, 18, 19, 20, 21.

So, at redemption and the resurrection of immortality we shall be without sin to serve the living God according to 1st Corinthians 15: 53, 54, 55, 56, 57. Here only sin brings death and not able to govern a planet being a world leader guiding all of humanity who if not all are sinners. And still in the flesh being therefore subjected to the infection and inheritance of sin at birth according to Romans 5: 12, 13, 14, 15, 16, 17.

So please Lord forgive me for this Blaspheme of what I am about to express here. Also being our Lord and Majesty and the Lord who will grant us this planet for us to rule it by those who you resurrect into immortality that will be subjected to without sin after this resurrection and immortality and making them Kings and Priests and those in the flesh making some of them also Kings and Priests on earth in this One World Government of the God of the Authorized King James Version Bible according to Daniel 7:27 and Revelation 5: 10. And that your sacrifice Lord our Majesty is that your sacrifice and of your blood that was shed on the cross and died for our sins that saved us all of those who placed their trust in your statutes and Judgments according to Deuteronomy 11: 32.

And that our Lord Jesus Christ the son of God the Father who came to earth and was conceived and born in the flesh and was crucified for our sins and is worthy to bring vengeance or retribution to those who have sinned and who have rejected him according to 1st John 4: 2, 3, 4, 5, 6. And that nowhere in the Authorized King James Version Bible does it reveal or mention that Jesus Christ will come back by name and person will rule this world and being personally present in the flesh as God and going by the name of our Lord Jesus Christ; except to be worthy to execute vengeance against the evil in this world by destroying the evil armies and destroying the one world government of the Antichrist of this world at Armageddon according to Daniel 7: 26 and according to Revelation 19: 5, 6, 7, 8, 9, 10, 11, 12, 13, 14 ,15, 16, 17, 18, 19, 20, 21 and Revelation 5: 1, 2, 3, 4, 5, 6, 7, 8, 9, 10, 11, 12, 13 ,14. And also to protect the land of Israel and here Israel represents the whole world of humanity. And here God will Judge that Israel --- that has rejected God --- and save that Israel that trusted and believed in our Lord Jesus Christ our God.

Now the Authorized King James Version Bible says that our Lord and Saviour Jesus Christ will only execute vengeance on this planet and not rule it personally on earth according to John 1: 44, 45, 46, 47, 48, 49, 50, 51, but to rule us all from his heavenly abode, (here the term "son of man" refers to a human being and refers not only to Jesus Christ but to possibly another human being also that may be born without having any guile as Christ has had and as he has mentioned in John 1: 47. And that Christ may have had also a more severe degree of having absolutely no guile.

As I have also have mentioned as well in this specific scripture of this explanation of John 1: 48 ,49, 50, 51 in detail in my other two books called "Pyromancy" and "Magistrates of Damnation" of this follower of Christ ruling this world after being accepted by humanity or if not accepted will rule the world after the government of the Antichrist is destroyed by Christ our God.

Where here God the Jesus Christ our Lord and Saviour will only come back in vengeance as I have mentioned here in this chapter against the evil armies at Armageddon according to Revelation 19: 5, 6, 7, 8, 9, 10, 11, 12, 13, 14, 15, 16, 17, 18, 19, 20, 21. And that our Lord Jesus Christ will not rule this world personally here on earth but to have that supreme authority to rule us all including the world leader of this one world government of the God of the Authorized King James Version Bible in this world and rule this world and all of us and our world leader from his heavenly abode. And then pass down to us this world and then grant us this world for us who have been resurrected by God into immortality without sin and to share and rule it with those who have also placed their trust in our Lord and Saviour Jesus Christ being in the flesh and having no immortality and being subjected to sin in the flesh being only mere mortals.

So, who will this human being be who is without any guile as Christ has mentioned in John 1: 47? He may be someone picked by God to rule this planet and where his rule on this planet will be subjected to and supervised under the supreme authority of God and our Lord Jesus Christ who was God in the flesh who came to die on the cross 2,000 years ago or so for our sins. And where God who is our Jesus Christ our Lord and his supreme authority will be executed from his heavenly abode, since it will only be that some of us who will be Kings and Priests onto our God; and for those only to reign on earth who were faithful to God and our Lord Jesus Christ according to Revelation 5: 10.

All of my books regarding these atrocities that have taken place recently and leading our world to the consummation of this age have now been written and published along with this 6th book " Genocidal Peace, " also to be published according to Isaiah 30: 8 in order to get the message across to an evil world that has caused chaos. As we are all guilty of this chaos and trusting in oppression and perverseness and that stays there on. And becoming a breach ready to fall as those infidels of the Bible or who are of the Egyptian God's of humanism like Trump and Putin who sit still while they shall help in vain and to no purpose shall not bring peace like the Barter System to eliminate digital monetary currencies or this one world digital currency or known as the Mark of the Beast but bring destruction according to 1st Timothy 6: 8, 9, 10 and Revelation 13: 14, 15, 16, 17, 18 and Isaiah 30: 7, 8, 9, 10, 11, 12, 13.

Also, to rule this planet you must have a spirit of flesh that God gives you instead of a stony heart which refers to a heart that plummets or lacks courage which I have now or fails where being very sociable is not possible with a stony heart. Here the term "stony" refers to "plummet" also "to build; a stone" also "having a heart with" divers weights" etc. as God may build up my spirit to a spirit of flesh in order to fight off my enemies according to the Strong's Exhaustive Concordance of the Bible of the Old Testament of # 68 from the root of # 1129. Here having a stony heart you have a lack of courage where you fail on a social level after being an outcast according to Jeremiah 30: 17. And having a heart of flesh you are able to fight off the most dangerous enemies and then being accepted by those heathens who are very or extremely sociable and who are extreme extroverts according to Psalms 18: 32, 33, 34, 35, 36 ,37, 38, 39, 40, 41, 42, 43, 44, 45, 46, 47, 48, 49, 50. So having a stony heart you cannot prevail by being able to fight off your enemies or be socially accepted. I have that stony heart right now until the resurrection takes place then I will have a heart of flesh.

That here after God gives you a heart of flesh you are able to walk in the statutes and judgments of God to execute these statutes and judgments and bring in that one world government of the God of the Authorized King James Version Bible with the help of other followers of Christ or the converts who may also be those heathens of and according to Psalms 18: 43. And as mentioned of the statutes and Judgments of Ezekiel 11: 17, 18, 19, 20, 21. Does God give this heart of flesh along with an immortal body to a servant chosen to rule this planet ? To be an actual and only Potentate and to be the King of kings and Lord of Lords where no man can approach this man of immortality that rules by power of spirit and immortality according to 1st Timothy 6: 14, 15, 16? But is this my fate sealed here?

Or is my fate instead sealed here that will I be burned alive according to Ezekiel 21: 31 in a land that I don't know now or years from now or be not familiar with that land like this land of celebrities and political entities. Or be chastised in a furnace by the kindling of fire. And in this furnace where I may be subjected to burning where I would be at the same time --- that I start to burn that I will be delivered and resurrected into immortality by God or redeemed by God from that furnace according to:

Ezekiel 21: 31 "And I will pour out mine indignation upon thee, I will blow against thee in the fire of my wrath, and deliver thee into the hand of brutish men, and skillful to destroy."

Ezekiel 21: 32 "Thou shall be fuel to the fire; thy blood shall be in the midst of the land; thou shalt be no more remembered; for I the Lord have spoken it." Or will I be chastised in that Furnace and then be delivered?

And will I be chastised by a kindling fire in that furnace and be delivered or be redeemed out of the hand of the "terrible" or the "tyrannical dictators" according to: Jeremiah 15: 14 "And I will make thee to pass with thine enemies into a land which thou knowest not: for a fire is kindled in mine anger, which shall burn upon you."

Jeremiah 15: 21 "And I will deliver thee out of the hand of the wicked, and I will redeem thee out of the hand of the terrible."

The term "terrible" according to The Strong's Exhaustive Concordance of the Bible # 6184 and from # 6206 refers to " fearful " i.e. powerful or tyrannical --- " mighty, oppressor, " In great power, strong, terrible, violent. Or is my fate also sealed here as in this scenario here as Hollywood movie star Samuel L. Jackson said in a speech, either in a movie or in real life possibly as well, and as God says as well in his word according to:
Ezekiel 25: 7 "Behold, therefore I will stretch out mine hand upon thee, and will deliver thee for a spoil to the heathen: and I will cut thee off from the people, and I will cause thee to perish out of the countries; I will destroy thee; and thou shalt know that I am the Lord."

Am I a moth in a house like in a psychiatric institution being totally reclusive and incarcerated because of writing these books and writing all these emails and letters to all the celebrities and political entities for years on this planet producing enemies everywhere on this planet? Whereas my incarceration is also as a booth that my keepers or psychiatrists who have incarcerated me have made? And will I be hissed out of my place or to be uttered at angrily and threatened out of my place of peace that I am in now? According to Job 27: 18, 19, 20, 21, 22, 23?

But did I forsake this life for Christ? And am I last or first in this world? Notice how it also refers to the Son of man and not the literal name of "Jesus Christ" that shall sit in the throne of his glory, since the term "Son of man" refers to a human being in the flesh and not just specifically "Jesus Christ" who was that Son of man who was conceived by the Holy Ghost and then born in the flesh and was crucified by the world for the sins of humanity, according to Matthew 19: 27, 28, 29, 30 and Galatians 6: 14, 15, 16, 17, 18 and Romans 9: 6, 7, 8, 9, 10, 11, 12, 13, 14, 15, 16. Here God raises up his servants and that his servants have God's power in his servants and for his servants to declare God's name throughout the whole earth according to Romans 9: 17 and Judges 2: 16, 17, 18, 19.

And who will take that crown that God will give to rule this planet according to Ezekiel 21: 25, 26, 27?

So, who will rule this planet instead of Jesus Christ as God in the flesh who only comes back in vengeance against his adversaries? That remains to be seen according to John 1: 44, 45, 46, 47, 48, 49, 50, 51.

Credits and Acknowledgements

I would like to thank our Lord Jesus Christ and God for the Scofield Authorized King James Version Study Bible and the Editors of this Bible like Rev. C.I. Scofield, D. D. and Rev. Henry G. Weston (President Crozer Theological Seminary) and Rev. James M. Gray, D.D. (President Moody Bible Institute) and Rev. Williams J. Erdman, D.D. (Author Gospel of John, etc., etc.) and Rev. Arthur T. Pierson, D. D. (Author, Editor, Teacher) and Rev. W. G. Moorehead, D.D. (President Xenia (U.P.) Theological Seminary) and Rev. Elmore Harris, D.D. (President Toronto Bible Institute) and Rev. Arno C. Gaebelein, D. D. (Author "Harmony of Prophetic Word," etc., etc.) and Rev. William I., Pettingill, D. D. (Author, Editor, Teacher).

And I would like to thank the editors of the Strong's Exhaustive Concordance of the Bible by James Strong, S.T.D., LL.D. and I also want to thank and show my gratitude to One Media Creative publishing which gave me the opportunity to make my books more appealing in the way the book covers of these books I have written were done. In not only the book covers but their formats and of the layout of these books done by the editors at One Media Creative.

And where Kate Rodriguez of One Media Creative publishing was a very big help in improving my books over all work which helped to inspire me to write my five following books except "Pyromancy." But inspired me with these other following five books called "Open Tomb, Aviation 666, Monsters of Genesis" and "Magistrates of Damnation" and "Immunity from Prosecution" and "Ancient Blood of Violence" and this 6th book I have written that you are now holding called "Genocidal Peace."

I would also like to thank all these following editors and journalists of the news Media. Analysis by John Blake, (CNN Sunday July 24 / 2022) and Kristin Kobes Du Mez and Philip Gorski, a Sociologist at Yale University and Co-author of: The Flag and the Cross: The Threat to American Democracy." Wikipedia "Roman Temple" and "J. Krishnamurti" (Is God an Invention of Thought) and Grace College (Biblical studies vs. Theology: What is the difference?) and "The Urantia Book Fellowship" and "The Straits Times": (1.4 trillion dollars lost to scams globally; Singapore victims lost on the average) and The Church of Latter Day Saints (Revelation Chapters 17- 18) and Pressbooks (Revelation explained) and Beyond Today ("What is the Difference between Sheep and Goats?) and Independent ("why did Russia invade Ukraine?") and The Toronto Star : Staff Reporters Ben Cohen and Joshua Chong ("World of Emotions") and CTV News CNN's Kaanita Iyer, Daniel Dale, Marshall Cohen, Veronica Stracqualursi , Jim Acosta, Kevin Liptar, and Matin Goillandeau (World news : Trump says he would encourage Russia to do whatever the hell they want…) and CNN business (Opinion : Fani Willis and Nathan Wade need to step aside for the sake of the country) and University of Virginia School of Law (Can presidents be prosecuted or sued ? Professor explains differing visions of immunity) and Harvard University Weatherhead (Center for international affairs defeating desperate dictators) and The New York Times Jennifer Valentino- Devries and Michael H. Keller and Maria Abi- Habib and Annie Correal and Jack Nicas and Ian Buruma and Tali Sharot and Cass R. Sunstein and Jessica L. Tracy University of British Columbia and Richard W. Robins University of California, Davis (The Psychological Structure of Pride: A tale of two facets) and Newsweek Emma Nolan (on John Lennon's assassination) and The Guardian "Lois Beckett."

‐‐‐‐‐‐‐‐‐‐‐ **John Bazzanella** ‐‐‐‐‐‐‐‐‐‐ Dated on Monday April 15th / 2024

www.ingramcontent.com/pod-product-compliance
Lightning Source LLC
LaVergne TN
LVHW011950070526
838202LV00054B/4877